The
LONELY
SEAT

If Business Was Easy,
Everyone Would Have One

KEITH TRUBSHAW

Published by Best Seller Publishing®, St. Augustine, FL
Best Seller Publishing® is a registered trademark.
Printed in the United States of America.

ISBN: 978-1-959840-60-2

This publication makes no claim to be anything other than a subjective narrative of the author's life and experiences. It is sold with the understanding neither the author nor the publisher are engaged in rendering legal, accounting, or other professional advice. If legal advice or other expert assistance is required, the services of a competent professional should be sought. The opinions expressed by the author in this book are not endorsed by Best Seller Publishing® and are the sole responsibility of the author rendering the opinion.

For more information, please write:
Best Seller Publishing®
53 Marine Street
St. Augustine, FL 32084
or call 1 (626) 765-9750
Visit us online at: www.BestSellerPublishing.org

CONTENTS

Everyone Wants a Piece of Me

Am I the font of all knowledge? The answer is no.
The source of all good things? It's once again no.
Yet when I walk through the doors, my life's not my own.
Even before that, just sitting at home
At the end of a phone call or email or text,
Beware of incoming from someone who's vexed
At a problem they have, they think's yours to solve
No matter the subject, no matter the time
It steals from your day, you're at their command.
It all comes your way, no matter your plans.

Forget about living the life of your dreams,
It's no longer your own is the way that it seems.
So often it's real, this weight that you carry
Unable to stop, unable to tarry
To chat to a colleague like you once did
For now you're the boss, so no longer their friend.
You're the one with the answers, and power over all
Yet inside you're the same, bewildered and small.
But this can't be a sham, it's your name over the door,
You wanted it, you got it, The Lonely Seat's yours.

All those around you, no longer the same,
They call you the boss but time and again,
You are their servant to help them along.
You find yourself wishing they'd sing their own song.
The orchestra is there, it's yours to conduct
If you get it wrong, then everyone's cooked.
But who can you turn to for a moment of peace
Free of demands and the gripes and the beefs?
Just for a moment, to regain who you are,
A human, just being, not some superstar.

Take time from your day to give to yourself,
To recharge your battery, to take time to smell
The roses around you, so long forlorn
From neglect and no-nurture because you have been torn
From the path that is yours to meet others' needs.
Did you sign up for this when you planted the seed?
Find someone to talk to, be someone who'll listen
With no hidden agenda, or judgemental derision,
Someone who's been there, who knows what it's like.
Reset the chess board, regain your life.
Do that, and it's better the boss you will be,
Then the better the business, set yourself free.

Everyone wanting a piece of you for themselves
Will always be so, as long as you are around.
Be brave and push them from the nest so to fly.
Maybe pain in the short term, but the rewards are so high.
You'll regain your life, yet still show that you care,
Finding balance and happiness is why The Lonely Seat's there.

—Keith Trubshaw

Dedication

I refuse to make this dedication a long, drawn-out affair that no one ever reads. So it will be short.

Firstly, this book is dedicated to all of those who told me to give up ... that I would never succeed. Thank you for spurring me on.

Secondly, to all those who did me wrong. Thank you for making me stronger.

Thirdly, this book would probably never have been completed if it wasn't for Mark Layder's encouragement that it could make a difference to so many.

But most importantly, it is dedicated to Graham Mathers, who changed my life with a single sentence, to Derek Church, my second dad, and Gary Brown, the best friend I ever had. Whatever I did, I could not have done it without you. Thank you.

PREFACE
If Business Was Easy, Everyone Would Have One

Do you know any millionaires? Do you know anyone who used to be a millionaire but lost their money? What about becoming a millionaire twice and losing it both times? Three times? I managed to do it four times! Getting to be a 'millionaire' wasn't that difficult, and it became a good deal easier as inflation took its toll. It was hanging onto that status that I wasn't so good at.

To lose a fortune once or twice is unfortunate, but to lose it four times takes a degree of expertise! That's nothing to brag about, is it? On the other hand, I guess that I did well to succeed four times in the first place. Success is a great teacher, but with the benefit of hindsight, I know that failure is a better one: this is a strong refrain throughout this book.

I have often described my career as a rollercoaster. In fact, it was more like a mirror image of what we see in theme parks, where the slow, rather unexciting climb to the top is something that we have to go through to experience the thrill of the descent. In business, however, the thrill is in the climb. The last thing you want is to experience the descent, for 'thrilling' it is certainly not. Unpleasant, stressful, traumatic or even terrifying would be a far better way of describing it. On a real rollercoaster, the gap between terrifying and thrilling is a fine line; exposing ourselves to the terror is the price we pay for the thrill. We know that it will soon come to an end and we will be fine, but on the business rollercoaster we don't know when it will end, and there's no gaurantee that we will be fine and undamaged when it does. And just like in the theme park, on the business rollercoaster, whatever we do, eventually the descent will come. Cases of everlasting growth are few, if any. Descent is always somewhere on the horizon, all we can do is hope that the descent isn't too terrifying. Your demise might be sudden, vertical and out of control, or it might be more gentle and well managed, but chances are, 'exciting' would not be a word you would ever use to describe it.

And what of those who are sure that they and their organisation are insulated against such things? Look at some of the huge companies that existed a hundred years ago, and you will find that barely any have survived, and of those that did, many are a shadow of their former selves.

Let's not forget descent also happens on a personal level. The eternal-life pill has yet to be perfected. The challenge is to enjoy the climb but at the same time create a structure that might just control the descent when it comes. Any trapeze artist will admit that they can be much more adventurous when they have a safety net to ensure a soft landing. It's the same in business — even though we may never use it, a safety net can significantly reduce our fear and stress levels. Doctors tell us that stress is a people killer, but it is also a killer of business, with its cold fingers creeping into every decision.

We never think of the stress when we start out. No bowing and scraping to wicked bosses: freedom to do what we want, when we want and more money than we know what to do with. That's the dream of running your own business. But anyone who has ever been in business knows that to be more the exception than the rule. The world of running a business is much more likely to be one of long hours, high stress and questionable rewards, but still, we do it. Why? Why, when it comes at such a high price, one that is paid not just by us but, all too often, by those around us whom we love and purport to care about, who have had to take a back seat for weeks, months, years or even a lifetime? Let me re-purpose the old adage of 'Behind every successful man, there is a successful woman' to 'Behind every successful person, there is a success-ful partner'. Whichever way it's put, I disagree. The way I see it is that behind every successful man or woman, if there is anyone at all, there is a *tolerant* partner.

The boss's chair is sometimes the best seat in the house, but then there are occasions when we would gladly give it away, if only we could find someone to share the burden. The trouble is, they never seem to appear when we need them. Our only option is to get on with it as best we can.

We can teach accounting, architecture, plumbing or plas-tering. In fact, we can teach almost anything, but one thing that can never be taught is what it's like to sit in the boss's chair. Nothing can prepare us for that day when we can no longer pass a problem upstairs, because *we are the upstairs*. There may well be advisers around us who are well meaning and, hopefully, of the highest calibre, but it is with us where the buck stops. Hence the term 'Lonely Seat' — the best seat in the house, otherwise why do so many strive to get there? But sometimes it lives up to its name and becomes a very lonely place to be.

Around the world, managing directors and business owners feed more people than all of the NGOs and charities put together. Who helps *them* while millions of employees rely on them to put bread on the table? Small- and medium-sized businesses are the biggest employers by far and carry huge responsibility, for which they are given little credit. They simply *get on with it*.

I make no pretence that this book is science-based; it's simply a collection of lessons I learned over the years and stories of how I survived and sometimes thrived. Mostly I was flying by the seat of my pants and probably got it wrong as many times as I got it right. Many of my actions were instinctive but years later, and much to my surprise, turned out to have been based on sound psychological or scientific principles.

My son called to say that there was an error on my LinkedIn profile; instead of describing myself as a business 'analyst', I'd made a typo and called myself a business 'analqst'. I called him back to say that I'd changed it into something more appropriate: business 'anarchist'. That's exactly what I am, a business anarchist. The rigours and rules of entrepreneurship and business are not for me. Rule-following is painting by numbers; I prefer to let creativity flow. General Douglas MacArthur said, 'You're remembered for the rules that you break'. In my eyes, conformity leads to mediocrity, at best. If I have to defy bullshit rules to break new ground, so be it.

Another trait on my LinkedIn profile needs another story to explain it. I use the term 'Man of Joy', which came out of a conversation with a friend. She had asked me what this book was to be about.

'The loneliness of leadership and how to survive it', I replied. 'I'm calling it "The Lonely Seat"'.

'That's a bit of a dowdy title for someone like you, Keith. You're my Man of Joy', she said.

Wow! What a wonderful thing for someone to say about you. I understood why she said it because I go around trying to make light of things, making people laugh when I can and generally having a good time. I believe that smilers are winners, but I'd never thought of myself in that way before. Man of Joy has become the inscription I'd like on my gravestone.

So, that's me: consultant, business anarchist, but most of all, Man of Joy. It has to be said though, my wife finds the title quite amusing.

'Man of Joy? You're a grumpy so-and-so', says she. Oh well, we can't have everything. All I can say is that if Man of Joy is what they say about me when I'm dead and gone, I'll take it.

The writer Joseph Campbell said, 'We are all seeking the experience of being truly alive'. Maybe that's the reason I started out in business for myself in the first place. I saw only the good things: the money, the lifestyle, the yachts, planes and fancy cars, but perhaps, above all else, the freedom to be me. I paid scant regard to the fact that it would take hard work and dedication, the prize in my imagination was too big to resist. Its calling was louder than all of the obstacles and nay-sayers that stood in the way. Working for myself meant that my destiny was finally to be in my own hands. I could work as hard as I chose, for as many or few hours as I wanted. I would be free . . .

Yeah. Right!

Some of those ambitions proved to be an illusion, but could they have been a reality if I'd known then what I know now? There is a recurring theme in this book: success is a great teacher, but failure is a better one. Failure marks out a pathway that I only discovered *after* I walked beyond it, all too often having taken a more difficult and sometimes dangerous route. **Too many businesses launch in pursuit of a big financial prize, only to founder on the rocks of poor reasoning.** Rather than money, our motivation should be a higher calling.

Eleanor Roosevelt said, 'Far and away, the best prize that life has to offer is the chance to work hard at work worth doing'. One way of making sure that we do work that's worth doing is to work for ourselves, with no one standing over us to dictate how we do it. Money and status are great motivators, but their beauty rapidly fades. Money is not sufficient as a 'why' if we are to stay the course for the long term. There has to be something more, something stronger.

You may read this and agree wholeheartedly. More likely, you will think that it doesn't apply to you — that you are different and that the money and status will drive you until you are in your old age. Maybe you're right; only time will tell. Perhaps one day you will revisit this book, maybe decades from now, brush off the dust and say, 'Blimey, he was right!' Hindsight is a wonderful thing, and at my age, I have more of it than most. It's part of that irreplaceable thing called 'experience'. Experience can't be taught; it is (hopefully) wisdom gathered through having encountered things in our past which help us get through situations in our present. It's experience that keeps us calm when the going gets tough because we know we have travelled a similar road before and lived to tell the tale. It allows us to see things with a different perspective and with the confidence that the problems we may face are not insurmountable. It's the bad, scary or difficult situations that count most in our experience locker. Almost anyone can swim in a calm sea, but how do they cope when the going gets rough and the waves are crashing over their head, when they find themselves in The Lonely Seat?

Experience allows us to come up with a solution when it might seem at first that everything is set against us. If we have travelled this way before, then our situation holds less fear, and the quality of our decision-making will be much better for it. In this book, I am going to share my successes and failures in life and business so that you might reflect on them as you create your safety net that will protect you from a serious fall from The Lonely Seat. Battle-scarred I may be, but I'm still here to tell the tale, *my tale*, and if it helps you to be optimistic that you can forge a better future, then I will have succeeded.

1

Creativity and Courage

Einstein believed that everything we see in this world was once imagined. Someone has to conceive of an idea before it can come into existence. Creativity lies at the heart of everything. But **as soon as stress or fear walks through the door, creativity jumps out of the window**, and with it any chance of future success.

In 2010, IBM surveyed 1,500 chief executives from around the world. Almost 60 percent of those surveyed cited creativity as the most important leadership quality needed to achieve success in business. Creativity, not simply within business but in life itself, offers solutions which would otherwise sail by unheeded as we strive with our noses pressed to the unimaginative grindstone.

On the other hand, fear is arguably the single biggest obstacle to progress in all walks of life. The fear mode that we slip into is born of our ancestors from thousands of years ago. It is the fight-or-flight instinct we revert to whenever we encounter danger. As far as I know, there are no sabre-toothed tigers lurking around the corner these days.

EXCITEMENT STARTS AT THE EDGE
OF THE DIVING BOARD

Fear is designed to keep us alive, not to stop us from making decisions because we might feel embarrassed if we get them wrong. Fear is constantly trying to stop us from doing hardly anything except breathe. *Excitement starts at the edge of the diving board.* Overrule the fear and take the leap. Chances are you'll grow your wings on the way down, and if you don't, let me know if you find any sabre-toothed tigers down there in the lunch queue.

That said, it's no surprise that we get more conservative as our business grows, because we have more to lose. We spend much of our time and effort trying to hang onto what we've got.

Some of my best creativity was at times when I had nowhere to go. When the only way was to take the leap, anything was better than the position I was in. Those are the times when decisions are easy, when the fear can be easily outweighed. The trick is to be able not so much to outweigh the fear, but to see fear for what it is: a way to keep us safe in our comfort blanket, a very effective way to stop us from moving forwards.

In my time, I have enjoyed the highs of success and felt the devastation of profound failure, and if there's one thing I have learned in my rollercoaster business life, it is this: **success is a great teacher, but failure is a better one!**

This book is not based upon academic theory but upon hard-won, often bitter, experience. If I had only known when I started out that all of my future screw-ups would be opportunities in the making, The Lonely Seat would have been far less lonely. I hope that reading my words will help you realise that you are not alone. Others have passed this way before and lived to tell the tale. If you are between a rock and a hard place, this will be a tough pill to swallow: what you're going through is necessary, even critical for growth. If we aren't growing, then we are stagnating, and in the world of business, stagnation is a precursor to death.

Fear of failure stops some people before they've even begun. The world is full of people who are about to set up their own business; but, if you meet them in a year, nothing's changed. They're 'waiting for the right time'. Then there are others who would love to set up a business of their own, but they are honest enough with themselves to admit that they lack the necessary guts to do so.

And that's what it takes — guts, balls, chutzpah. But here's the thing: there are thousands of businesses formed because the owners simply couldn't get a job. Indeed, that was how some of my businesses came about. Who wanted to employ the managing director of a failed business? If I had been on the other side of the Atlantic, where previous failures are often regarded as a badge of honour and almost a prerequisite for acceptance into many roles, then things might have been different, but I wasn't, so it was a case of just getting on with it.

Generally, the UK view is that a failure in the past will surely lead to failure in the future. This approach has left countless organisations bereft of talent. Had they bothered to look beyond their cosseted boardrooms, they might have spotted someone sweeping the streets who could have been their salvation.

Having a business takes capital (often more than you think), demands great sacrifice (definitely more than you think) and requires commitment by the bucketload. But most of all it takes courage to walk to the edge of the cliff and jump. Courage to accept that there is a chance that you will fail and crash, and the belief that if you do, you will be able to pick yourself up and start again. Yes, you might well be worse off than if you had never jumped, if you had hung on to that precious day job, but at least you tried, and that deserves respect. I say *deserves* respect, and that is generally what you will get from those who have been there. The majority, however, will judge you as, at best, a failure and, at worst, a criminal. Business demands risk; that's how profit is generated. The government and media smile upon those who forge paths and become high-flyers, holding them up as examples of how wonderful this country is. One minute you will be rubbing shoulders with smiling politicians who are keen to bask in your glory, but get it wrong and you won't see them for dust.

Grow a thick skin. You might not need it now, but you will need it before the game is over, and you'll certainly need it if you crash and burn, especially if you have the audacity to pick yourself up to start again: just because you have failed, doesn't make you a failure.

You haven't failed until you give up.

Some of my businesses were more successful than others. Several failed, some spectacularly so. Do I see myself as a failure? Nope. Today, I am successful, and I lead a great life. I like to think that I have learned from my mistakes. I won't claim that to fail again holds no fear for me, but I have been there before and learned enough to know that it will be survivable.

COURAGE TO LET GO AND BE DIFFERENT

For decades, I was convinced that money was all I needed. The more I had, the happier I'd be. I went through life with clenched fists, trying to hold on to every last penny. I had to lose not one, not two or even three, but *four* fortunes before I finally learned my lesson.

Wealth cannot be captured; it is liquid and takes the form of whatever contains it. Clenched fists leave no room inside. Open hands can hold much more. When I finally embraced this, my life became easier almost overnight, my Lonely Seat . . . less lonely.

Think of it this way. If you spend your life preventing anything you possess escaping, then you have caged what you have. But cages also keep things out. While you are desperately hanging on to what you have, so much more is passing you by.

All my life I have chosen a different path. Sometimes I crashed to the ground, but other times I soared against all the odds. Every previous attempt I have made writing this book stalled because I tried to go by the rules. So, I am just going to tell my story, my way. I hope that by doing so, one or two of you might be inspired to go out there, walk to the edge of the diving board and take that leap of faith that you CAN do it. You CAN make a difference in the world. If you're at the bottom with nowhere to go, and this book gives you renewed optimism, thinking, 'If that idiot Keith can do it, so can I', then I have succeeded.

2

First Steps

Mine was a school like any other, a place where some teachers are better than others. Some knew their subject inside out, while others seemed only a page or two ahead in the textbook. The best teachers stand out head and shoulders above their colleagues because they have the ability to engage and enthuse their pupils. Teachers are well aware of the influence and responsibility they carry, but they are also humans who have good days and bad days.

Here is an example of someone who was having a bad day.

Mathematics came relatively easily to me. As a six-year-old, it had suddenly seemed to click into place during a one-on-one session with the wonderful Miss Biggs. But suddenly there I was in my second year at senior school, in a maths lesson with a teacher who was not succeeding in endearing me to his subject. He had marked an equation on the blackboard and spotted that my attention was elsewhere. To prove his suspicion, he fired a question at me. I was caught out, unable to answer correctly. He angrily asked the question again, as though repeating it would impart some new knowledge to his pupil. I got it wrong again. He called me up to the front of the class and went through what he had been telling us earlier. But this time it was delivered impatiently, and directly to me. Even though I was supposed to be good at maths, by now I was nervous and ridiculed; I still didn't 'get it'. He asked me again, and I realised I must have got the answer wrong again, as his hand connected with the back of my head. He asked me again and again, and each time my wrong answer resulted in my being struck. He had lost it. These were not just taps — they were full, open-handed slaps that he delivered as hard as he possibly could.

The whole class had fallen into stunned silence. In those days, some corporal punishment was allowed to maintain discipline, but this went far beyond what was acceptable. Every blow sent me stumbling against the blackboard. He was hitting me as though he felt he could knock the ability to answer the question into the back of my head. Looking back, he was taking his frustration out on me, a twelve-year-old boy who couldn't answer his question. I was so terrified when I pointed to what I hoped would be the correct answer that my hand shook. He didn't even tell me I was wrong. *Thwack*! Another blow did his talking for him.

That was more than fifty years ago, and you may wonder why I am telling the story. Don't get me wrong, my life wasn't in danger, but with the blows he was delivering, my fear of the next one was so profound that there was no chance of me thinking through the process that would have delivered the correct answer. We talked about fear in the last chapter, and everyone's fear of failure comes from somewhere — perhaps even an incident like this!

What I did not know as a twelve-year-old, and what my teacher apparently didn't know either, is that when we are in fear, our ability to apply even the simplest logic deserts us.

I hope the vivid memory of that encounter made me a better boss, showing me that anyone who is in fear of making the wrong decision is likely to do just that.

How many bosses, in one way or another, are guilty of making their staff feel ridiculed and small? Could it be that they treat people that way simply *because they can*?

We have all heard the expression: 'Be nice to people you meet on the way up, because you are likely to meet them on the way down'. If we behave badly to those around us so that they only do as we wish out of fear, then they will either not do it, or if they do, they will not do it as well as they might have because of the fear and stress they are under. And here is something else to consider: when we are no longer in the position we were, when we find ourselves on the greasy pole of descent, will they reach out to help us? Why the heck should they?

After having failed to knock the answers into the back of my head, my teacher demanded that I seek him out the next day, saying that I'd better have the correct answer for him. The next morning, I found him in the corridor and produced my exercise book in which I had worked out the problem for myself. He could not have been nicer. 'Well done', he said, benignly. Over the two years that he taught me, that was the only time he was nice to me. He actually smiled. Maybe he realised that he had gone too far on the previous day. He didn't knock me around because I was too stupid to answer his questions. He did it because he had allowed his anger to get the better of him. I suspect that he was in a Lonely Seat of his own, for Lonely Seats aren't just to be found in the boss's office. Life can get on top of anyone.

That episode was the lowest point in what were otherwise five happy years at school. Now let me tell you about the highest point — maybe not at the time, but now, fifty years later, a moment that I would not change for the world.

DICKIE'S STORY

I didn't know, or it hadn't perhaps registered, that his name was Graham. To the boys of Bilston Grammar School, he had been affectionately bestowed with the name 'Dickie'. He was still in his twenties when a motley crew of eleven-year-olds trooped into his classroom for the first time. He was to be our English Master. I think of him when I watch that fabulous film *Dead Poets Society*; Dickie could have been the man who inspired Robin Williams's character. I suspect he would be summarily dismissed nowadays for setting aside one lesson each week for a whole term to dramatically recount a story we had never heard of . . . J. R. R. Tolkien's *The Lord of the Rings*, even singing the eleven songs featured within its pages. I still remember it to this day, his university gown flowing behind him as he sang 'A Elbereth Gilthoniel' at the top of his voice. He lit a spark of wonder amongst his pupils (or one of them, at least) which would last a lifetime.

Sadly, Dickie was taken ill with a brain tumour. He was off work for a year, in which time we had a replacement teacher who was probably perfectly good at her job but didn't stimulate us like he did. Dickie finally returned with a long vertical scar running down from his hairline to his eyebrows. He had survived.

A short while after his return, I guess when he'd had a chance to bring himself up to speed with what his pupils had been up to, he called me into his study. It was barely bigger than a store cupboard, lined with shelves full of books, with a single chair, and a desk piled high with papers and homework. This is how the conversation went.

'Trubbers,' [that was his name for me — nicknames are a two-way street, I guess] 'what's happened to you?'

'What do you mean, Sir?'

'Your work has gone down the pan'.

'I don't like *her*, [the replacement teacher] Sir'.

'That's no excuse'.

And then he delivered it, the bombshell that was to define my life.

'Let me tell you something, young man. There are 300 boys in this school, and you are not the cleverest, not by a long way, but not one of them can touch your imagination'.

Perhaps he knew what he was doing when he said what he said, perhaps he didn't. Perhaps he was simply trying to get a fourteen-year-old, full-of-attitude Black Country kid to wake up. What I often wonder is this: did he realise the impact his words would have over fifty years later as I write this? Whether he believed it, whether or not it was true, didn't matter. I believed it; that was all that counted.

That single sentence lit something inside me, a flame that has sometimes dimmed when I have been under stress but never gone out. A flame that, because I believed him, I have fed all of my life. Years later, I tried to trace Dickie, just to say thank you for something he probably wouldn't have remembered. I was too late. After I told my story to a group of Rotarians, one of them, a doctor, approached me to say that Graham Mathers had died under his care in hospital. Bless you, Dickie, you changed my life.

In all of us a reservoir, of boundless creativity
Open up the sluice gate, set it free to flow
That sluice gate is not made of iron,
Or unyielding granite stone,
But forged within our mind from fear
Of falling, and being alone.

—*Keith Trubshaw*

And what is fear but '**f**alse **e**xpectations **a**ppearing **r**eal'?

REFLECTION

Almost every business problem we face can be best solved by getting creative, by conjuring up a solution from thin air. Creativity comes from imagination, the most important tool we can ever possess. We should value it and nurture it, not just in ourselves but in our children and those who look to us as the boss.

And what did I take from the trauma of being physically assaulted because I couldn't answer a question? In four decades of being a so-called boss, I've always guarded against robbing people of their confidence by scolding them, particularly in front of others.

As I write this, I am reminded of an incident I witnessed. I was meeting with the chief executive of a substantial business when he had to step out of his office to check on the progress of something or other. Through his open door, I heard him speaking to a someone, clearly an experienced member of his team.

Nevertheless, he scolded her for not coming up to the standards he required. He didn't shout, but everyone in the open plan office heard what he said. He probably thought that, as a boss, he was justified in saying what he did, and he was sure that she would not make the same mistake again. But what of her feelings? She would've been left feeling small, her self-esteem on the floor. She may well have done things his way thereafter, but any creativeness, so important in the rest of her job, would've been thrown down the toilet.

How much better would it have been to take her quietly to one side and go through the reasons that things should have been done differently, show her how valuable she was to the business and say that this was just a glitch that she could easily have corrected with his guidance? Maybe he could even have admitted his own error for not having made his wishes clearer in the past.

3

The Fourteen-Year-Old and the Merchant Banker

As I got older, the word *careers* started to loom on the horizon. Truth be told, I hadn't worked hard enough to be invited to carry on in the sixth form to do 'A' levels. In those days it was expected that grammar school pupils should become doctors or lawyers or accountants. I wanted none of those things. I drew a significant amount of ridicule when I declared I wanted to be a millionaire. I was having ideas beyond my station!

My year group was renowned for being troublesome as the years went by, more in a non-cooperating and boisterous way than a violent or malevolent one. Nonetheless, I think the teaching staff must have dreaded what we might have planned for the last day of school, so one afternoon they simply announced as we were leaving for the day that we needn't come back anymore. That was it — five years and no celebration. Onwards and upwards: millionaire status, here I come.

I have said that at school I declared my ambition as wanting to be a millionaire. Looking back, I realise that even then, at thirteen or fourteen years old, I was trying to do something about it. I had sent for a how-to booklet on setting up in business as a finance broker: *This is for me,* I thought! I read every word over and over, planning my way to a fortune. Then came the time for action. I didn't want to worry my mother with my entrepreneurial schemes. Her mantra was firmly 'neither a borrower nor a lender be', so I didn't use the phone at home.

Instead, I went to a call box . . . you know, one of those sites of historic interest nowadays. I dialled the number of what I believed to be a merchant bank called Gresham Trust and asked to speak to the managing director. Would you believe he took my call? I explained who I was and that I wanted to set up in business as a finance broker. I wanted to give his company the opportunity of providing the finance that I could re-lend to others.

He must have been grinning from ear to ear when he learned that this was a fourteen-year-old kid calling from a pay phone. But the thing is, he was nice to me, bless him; he certainly didn't have to be. He gave me his time, and to this day I thank him for it; if everyone treated everyone else the way he treated me, this world would be a nicer place. He said something along the lines of it not being the kind of market that his company was engaged in, then went on to suggest that I might want to finish off my schooling and get a job in the banking world so that I could learn the ropes properly before I set out on my own.

In honesty, I don't remember what he really said. My only memory is of that kindness towards me, and the words I have put into his mouth are, I like to think, ones which I might have used in similar circumstances years later. He didn't leave me deflated; in effect, he suggested I look to the longer term and keep trying.

Perhaps I wasn't deflated, because there was wisdom in his words. *We should lift our gaze from the very short term, onto the horizon.* How wonderful is that kind of advice for anyone who has ever tried to achieve anything? If we limit ourselves to only having a short-term goal, then any setback feels like a catastrophe. Yet that setback is not nearly so significant when we have our eyes on the horizon.

Put it this way: if you were on a journey towards a specific place one mile away and some unforeseen event knocked you back by another mile, it would be a big deal: your destination would now be twice as far away. But if your eyes had been on another, bigger destination a hundred miles away, you would only be one percent further away than you were before the setback. Short-term goals are great, but long-term goals keep things in perspective.

WELCOME TO THE WORLD OF WORK

The career guidance at school was, for me at least, as much use as a chocolate teapot. My mother told me that my careers counsellor had ridiculed my career choices as being far beyond *his* expectations of what I could achieve. I'm pretty sure she got a little annoyed and ended up defending me and my grandiose ambitions. But in one very important respect he was correct; I couldn't walk out of school and be a wealthy businessman overnight. I needed a job that would equip me for the road I wanted to follow.

In my naivety, I decided the best way to gain the kind of knowledge I needed was to get a job in an office. But in honesty, developing my commercial and business acumen wasn't the main reason an office job appealed. I wanted to wear a suit to work, look smart and not get my hands dirty. This was ironic on two fronts. First, I had a reputation amongst my friends' mothers as the kid they least liked their sons to play with because we always got involved in some new adventure and came home filthy. Second, I had worked in a market garden since the age of eleven, and my favourite task had always been muck spreading! It was a once-a-year task that took the best part of a Saturday.

The only mechanical aids were a shovel and a wheelbarrow. Gradually, the muck made its way up the sides of my wellingtons and onto my jeans. My mother made me get undressed in the backyard. Apparently, my appearance and smell were not to her liking! She dreaded the time of year when the job came around, but I loved it. Hour after hour, wheelbarrow load after wheelbarrow load. All day my imagination had me on my own farm. A farm! That is what I would do. That's how I'd make my fortune.

I have heard of others who, as prisoners of war forced to do back-breaking work, got through by transporting themselves elsewhere. Physically they were still doing the same job, and their captor's whip might have stung their back, but it could never reach their freedom of mind. I guess even as a youngster, I was reframing what I was doing, seeing it as a stepping stone to my ultimate goal. I was mapping my route to freedom whilst carrying out the most mundane of tasks. I lifted my eyes beyond the drudgery to the greater prize on the horizon. On those days, fatherless and almost penniless, I was as happy as I have ever been.

My first office job was as a commercial trainee (an apprentice without the status) at a steelworks. My first day included a tour of the head office, the highlight of which was a trip to a space-age air-conditioned building full of what looked like overgrown whirring tape recorders. The company's chief accountant proudly announced it as the brand new computer block. They had invested five million pounds in a computer the size of a tennis court with far less power than a cell phone. How time flies.

I was given a seat in the company's cost department, where I was introduced to a new-fangled device called an electronic calculator with which I was to spend the next year checking stores' requisitions (slips of paper handed into the stores in order to withdraw anything, from a roller bearing to a roll of toilet paper). No matter that some of the requisitions were clearly scurrilous; such things were above my pay grade. I had to make sure that the cost codes entered on them were the correct combination of digits to be entered into the new-fangled whirring tape device next door. Yuk! Boring, boring, boring, but my eyes were on the prize: I was there to learn.

I was given day release to study for an Ordinary National Certificate in business studies, which was the gateway for anyone who hadn't stayed on at school to enter professions like accounting. However, my acceptance onto the course was conditional on my successfully resitting my English Language O level, which I had flunked through not completing the comprehension exam. Certain that the examiners would be impressed by my clearly brilliant level of comprehension, I had been too busy writing in-depth answers to the first couple of questions to get to the final few. Luckily, the resit was under a different exam board, which used objective tests to judge the students' level of comprehension. Ticking boxes turned out to be something I was good at.

By and large, college was easy. No teachers breathing down my neck; it was my own choice whether I worked or not, which turned out to be just what I needed. I suddenly woke up. For the last five years, I'd been doing the barest minimum to keep my teachers off my back. At college it hit me: this education business, all of this learning, it wasn't for them . . . it was for me! Every lesson became a source of material or knowledge I could use in the future to set up my own business. Every dry theory became real. I worked my backside off and passed every subject with flying colours.

As testament to how I had changed, it occurred to me that there were 'O' and 'A' levels I could take in the same subjects I'd been studying, so I decided that I would take a few for a laugh. I passed them all except for A level law, which had a totally different syllabus, presenting me with questions that may as well have been in Greek. Sitting for an hour and a half, answering the questions I wished they'd have asked did me no good. It was a law exam, not politics. But there is a serious point here.

College was an environment where I thrived. Plant a tree in its ideal surroundings, and it will grow beyond your expectations. Humans are just the same; the difference between thriving and doing just enough to get by is all down to our environment. If you are a boss, and you learn that lesson early enough, you will be amazed at what your team will achieve. And *team* will be the word . . . your Lonely Seat may not be so lonely after all.

I found to my surprise that I was doing pretty well at college, but of all the subjects I studied, it was law that came most easily. I looked at what path that aptitude might open up for me and decided to study for the professional degree offered by The Institute of Chartered Secretaries and Administrators. Its exams demanded a high-level competency in accountancy and law, which didn't seem too daunting.

Best of all, English law required that every company had to have a company secretary, and when I looked at the job vacancies, the money looked good. But it wasn't a job I wanted. The need to set up my own business, to get to that magical million, was not just still there; it was steadily growing.

4

Selling Hand Grenades

I had only been working for a year or so when I made my first foray into setting up a business for real. Like many of my generation, countless happy hours were spent perusing what was on offer on the magazine shelves in newsagent shops (no, not the top shelves ... I wasn't tall enough). My eyes were often drawn to two publications. *Exchange and Mart* was, I guess, the eBay of its day, where everything from business opportunities to Pumas could be found. (Yes, I did say 'Pumas'. As I recall, they were £125.00 each — a lot to someone only earning £8.00 a week.) The other publication was *The Trader*, in which wholesalers and importers of the widest possible array of goods advertised their wares in bulk to those who might want to resell them.

I found a warehouse not too far from where I lived that seemed to have some interesting items, which I reckoned could help me return a tidy profit. I turned up at their door with my newly made-up business name and spent all I could afford on six identical items: heavy, die-cast cigarette lighters in the shape of hand grenades! (Not a product you would find on the market these days, I suppose. But hey, they were different times.)

With my product in hand, my dream of success now revolved around my ability to sell them. It began to dawn on me that just because I thought they were cool didn't necessarily mean that anyone else would share my opinion. I guess a kind of buyer's remorse had kicked in. Had I done the right thing? There was only one way to find out. I carefully wrote out my advertisement for the *Exchange and Mart*, keeping the number of words to a minimum so that I could afford to pay for it, then waited for publication day (Thursdays). Surely orders would come flooding in, and I'd have to go back to the warehouse and buy up all of their stock. However, none of my thousands of clients would be able to order by phone. The only way was to send an order through the post along with a cheque or postal order.

My first two orders finally arrived, and I posted the goods out that same day so that I would be ready for the deluge that would surely come the next day, or at worst the day after. But no more orders came. Ever. It seems the world hadn't shared my impeccable taste after all. I was left with four items unsold. A salutary lesson about not just choosing the right product but also pricing correctly.

I actually lost money on those two sales once I'd costed all of the time and effort that they took to create. There is a world of difference between gross profit and net profit, and it's the latter that counts. Given the negative ratio between work I'd put in (quite a lot) and the rewards I extracted (nil), I came to the decision that the world wasn't ready for Keith's mail-order empire just yet.

Today, everything would be different. Would my venture have made money in these times of instant response and next-day deliveries? Maybe, but chances are still no. Not for the commercial reasons you might imagine, but for the fact that if I followed the same product line today, I would most likely receive a visit from certain law enforcement authorities!

EVERY DOG HAS ITS DAY

The second year of my training period had been cut short. I was offered a full-time job in the company's buying office, working for a chief buyer who taught me a great deal and was never anything but kind to me, even when I had been in the wrong. His name was Ken Elwell, and I will always hold his memory with fond regard and respect. However, in my first year, one of the accounting bosses had been, on occasion, quite the opposite of kind. For that reason, I will not name him.

In fairness, my immediate boss, a fiery but fair Irishman called Pat Hanley, had remonstrated with the anonymous boss that young Keith should not be bullied. But in those days, the boss could do more or less as he wished with impunity, and I was not about to go running to *his* boss, so I had to grin and bear it or join the union. I chose the latter, which was no help, especially since I moved departments and thus out of my adversary's reach.

A few years later, however, I was invited to his office. It seemed that I was the only one on staff who was actually passing their exams. He thought I might like to come back to work in his department, as though it were some big prize. You can guess what my answer was. I kept it polite, but every dog has his day, right? To him, his mistreatment of me a few years earlier had been a non-event; he had forgotten it. **But here's the thing: it's not the bully but the bullied who is the judge as to whether bullying has taken place.** And when you're on the wrong end, it's not a nice place to be. I am not by nature a vengeful person, but if he had fallen to his knees and begged me to go back, the answer would still have been no. His department was short of much-needed talent for one reason: him.

It is strange how we remember, so many years later, apparently insignificant instances such as that. Yet as I write this, I realise that it is one of those instances that have influenced the way I treated my employees over the years that followed. I suppose it's kind of biblical to suggest that we should treat others as we would ourselves be treated.

All of that said, I didn't want to leave the buying office anyway. There, I was in contact with the outside world and able to use my imagination to develop ideas as to how I could set up in business for myself. One of my areas of responsibility was as a steel buyer. Perhaps that may seem odd, since we were a steel manufacturer, but there are all kinds of steel used in a heavy engineering factory with 1,800 employees. My contact with the steel-stockholding industry was beginning to shape what my future business would become.

But I guess there aren't many who have gone from assistant buyer to steel-stockholding tycoon in one easy step, so I had to bide my time.

Many professional buyers, who come face to face with salespeople on a daily basis, start to think they would make a good sales representative themselves. I was one of those people. My current job had become boring; I was well within my comfort zone. As I saw it, my career progression had been halted by a blue-eyed boy being inserted a couple of places ahead of me on my career path. It was time to move on.

At that time, my mother's advice was something along the lines of:

'Don't leave there, Keith. It's a secure job, and they are hard to find'.

The irony was that within three or four years, I was back there purchasing desks (my old one amongst them) at their closing down auction sale. Almost 2000 jobs lost, never to return.

That 'secure job' was an illusion.

I scoured the job vacancies and found an opening for a sales representative for a rubber and plastics distributor. I got the job, but after a month, I hated it. My boss, the sales director, was scandalously unkind. His secretary quietly admitted that she could not believe how badly he was treating me. But truth be told, I wasn't very good at the job. I was expected to sell products that were more expensive than our rivals', which might have been possible if we had been the best in terms of service; in fact, we were the worst. Customers were treated as though we were doing them a favour. Even after I persuaded a client to let us supply their needs for one particular product, the company's trade counter staff would tell them that we didn't sell such things.

One of our major product lines was safety gloves. Selling these door to door on cold rainy days was not my idea of fun, especially when I was expected to write a report on every client that I visited. On one particular day, I'd knocked on twenty-nine doors, waited in or outside twenty-nine reception areas, and failed to be allowed in to see a single buyer. The day was coming to a close, but there was one more door to be knocked. I walked into a grimy reception area and tapped on a closed hatch window. It slid back and a face appeared. I handed over my card and asked to see the buyer. He sighed one of those *here's someone else to waste our time* kind of sighs, turned away and walked to the back of the office. I was expecting him to be returning with the instruction that I should go away but, music to my ears, I heard his boss say that he would see me. I was invited in and stood in front of his cluttered desk.

'Trubshaw', he said, looking at my card.

'Yes', I replied hopefully.

'I knew someone by that name. He was a corporal in the Staffordshire Regiment. Was he your dad?'

Here I was thinking how the sales manuals tell us to build rapport. I was in!

'Yes, he made sergeant, so I assume he must have been a corporal at some stage'.

'Well, I thought I'd invite you in so that I could let you know . . . he was a right bastard! On your way, son'.

What a great way to end the day.

I am the kind of person who purposely leaves no room inside to hate anything or anyone. But that job and my boss came pretty close to being the exception.

I had jumped out of the frying pan and into the fire. I needed another job. Any job. I saw an advertisement for a steel buyer, which seemed to be made for me. There was no company car, but that didn't matter; I just needed to get out. It turned out that whilst a major part of the job was buying, the position was that of a general manager of a small steel-stock-holding business that sold mainly to its sister companies within an engineering group.

I was interviewed by the chairman of the group, who was the first millionaire I had actually met and shaken hands with. I couldn't have been too fazed by his status when I declared that he shouldn't employ me if he wanted someone to say *yes sir, no sir, three bags full, sir* to his every whim. If I thought he was wrong, I wouldn't be able to resist telling him so.

'That's just what I want', he said, and promptly offered me the job, which as it turned out came with a pay rise and a Ford Cortina.

I have met many chief executives. All claim that they are tired of people telling them only what they want to hear. Yet almost all, when push comes to shove, show the person who dares to question their decisions the door . . . funny, that.

If I'd hated my last job within a month of being there, this job was quite the reverse. I was in my element — buying, selling, negotiating and managing. Every moment was equipping me for the day when I would strike out on my own.

HITTING THE GROUND RUNNING

That chairman taught me a great deal, and I have much to thank him for. He had a ruthless streak that I will never possess, but it takes all kinds to make a world. On one occasion, when he thought I'd done wrong, he came down on me hard. I felt I had been treated unfairly and handed him my resignation effective six weeks hence, and used the time I was still there to prove myself innocent of what he had been told.

Before I left, he'd found out the truth of what had really happened and apologised to me. We parted as friends, which was an ideal outcome. He didn't invite me to reconsider, and I don't think I would have anyway. I had £300 in the bank and an old Austin Maxi worth another £300. It was the kick that I needed. I was in business and a company director at last.

Almost everyone who starts a new venture has done lots of planning, getting customers and suppliers lined up so that they hit the ground running. One April evening in 1980, I sat at home on the toilet and said out loud, 'What have I done?' (I wasn't looking down the toilet at the time!) I had no orders, no suppliers and just £300 to my name.

On May 1st 1980, I entered my new office in Dudley in the West Midlands. It had one chair, one desk and no phone.

Not the most auspicious of starts. The phone took nearly a week to arrive, so I spent my days trawling through the Yellow Pages in search of prospects who might want to take a chance on an upstart steel supplier.

Those first few days in that empty, silent office, though I did not know it at the time, were where the first seeds of The Lonely Seat were sewn.

When one of my stockholder friends who had started in business a year or so earlier had said, 'It's cold out here', I had never realised until then just how true his words were.

REFLECTION

There is an old adage that says failing to plan means planning to fail. I had no intention of failing, but I was trusting luck to a far greater extent than I realised at the time. I'd spoken to a few customers telling them of my plans. A few had wished me luck but made no promises that they would send orders my way. Others had promised they would give me lots of business because we were friends.

What do you think happened? The ones who promised the most delivered the least. Furthermore, as soon as my status within my former job was gone, they never accepted another call.

So, if you're about to start in business, take everything you are told with a pinch of salt. The moment you start out on your own, the dynamics of your relationship with both suppliers and customers will change. In my experience, those who promise the most will all too often deliver the least.

5

Big Kahunas

Business started slowly, but what I lacked in experience, I made up for with energy, enthusiasm, and in no small measure, tenacity. With my wife's help, I managed to get a £5,000 overdraft facility secured on our house and used the money to finance my first deal. It made £800 profit. I was up and running. My second deal was a straight back-to-back purchase and sale to the man who had said, 'It's cold out here'. He didn't pay me; the bank's £5,000 was gone. **Lesson: don't put all your eggs in one basket.**

But what choice did I have except carrying on? By now I'd gained a few contracts, and a small amount of credit was being extended to me. At that time, in that industry, you were only as good as what you could buy; the selling part was almost easy. I managed to gain credit from a large steel company who had long been my target. Knowing them as I did, they were going to be the mainstay of my trip to becoming a millionaire. All I had to do was make sure I paid them on time, and my credit line would steadily increase.

I bought my first batch of steel and resold it to a friend. But when payment day came around, he said I'd have to wait.

He had clearly decided that other suppliers were more important to his business. I had no choice but to be honest with my supplier. Once again, all my eggs had been in one basket: I could not pay them until he paid me. He did pay me in the end . . . a month late. I never got credit from that supplier again. All of my hopes had rested on that supplier, so it was back to the drawing board. To this day, that friend does not know just how much damage he did to my business. Have I told him? No. What would be the point? What good would it serve?

I sound as though I was going from disaster to disaster, and maybe I was, but we haven't lost until we give up, right? With the words 'small fishes are sweet' in my ears, I'd begun putting together a few suppliers and customers who were making me a small but steady living. Nevertheless, I wanted more, a lot more!

After just four months in business, I heard of a machine on the market that would enable me to do all of my own processing. I bought it and rented a four and a half thousand square foot factory to house it. Then, and only then, did I realise that I needed more money. The words *cash* and *flow* had reared their scary heads. I needed to increase my overdraft from £5,000 to £12,000 (maybe not much nowadays, but two year's wages back then). My bank manager's words stay embedded in my memory:

'You're asking me *after* you need it?'

'Er, yes'.

'Seems I have to back you or sack you . . . Go on then, you can have your money, but don't do this to me again'.

If you are going to be born with any trait, be born lucky. There's probably not a chance in hell that a conversation like that would take place in a bank manager's office today. I was a lucky boy.

I recruited a machine operator and started interviewing for the assistant he would need. Of all the candidates, one seemed nervous when I asked him questions:

'Can you read a micrometer?'

'Yes'.

'Can you read a vernier calliper?'

'Er . . . yes'.

I knew he was lying, but it endeared him to me. He wanted the job so much that he was willing to lie to get it. Not a profound untruth, just a white lie, and besides, it was an easy skill to teach. Phil stayed with me as a major player in my business for many years. Lovely man.

We worked like Trojans on a machine barely fit for the purpose, making do and mending as we went along. The factory had no office and the machine was noisy, so the telephone had to be in the toilet, but we were trading and producing quality products that customers liked.

REFLECTION

Employing Phil had been a matter of luck more than judgement. There were others more qualified, but because I liked him, I followed my instincts. We spend a lot of time with people we work with, so surely it's better to work with people we like. I know we can go too far in that regard and shouldn't employ people who are not up to the task, but having so often followed my head and employed people who were clearly the best in terms of technical ability, I learned that it is better to have someone who gets along with those around them than a so-called superstar who brings nothing but disharmony.

SIGN OR YOU'LL LOSE IT ANYWAY

We had been properly up and running for about a month. So far things were going well. There was an incoming steel delivery, and while I was checking it over, Gary, my next-door neighbour, also a steel stockholder, called in. We were walking through the factory when suddenly he looked over my shoulder and said: 'Watch out!'

Too late. As I stepped backwards, I tripped, and five tonnes of steel fell with a sickening *whump* across my legs.

There were three people under that steel. One was trying to organise some way of getting it off me, another was screaming in agony, and bizarrely, a third was thinking of the film *Jaws*, where one of the characters slid to the back of his boat into Jaws's jaws (that's a mouthful). All three of those people were me. The pain was beyond imagination. By some superhuman effort they pried up the steel enough to drag me clear.

It was the first time I had ever been in an ambulance. The hospital prodded and poked, and after numerous X-rays showed that I had broken my left foot and right leg, I heard a doctor send a message to the plasterers not to go home, as he had another patient for them.

'I don't know if this makes any difference, but I have private health insurance', I said through a mist of morphine. The next thing I knew, a consultant surgeon was at my bedside. Those health insurance words turned out to be the luckiest I have ever uttered.

'We are not putting *that* in plaster', he declared and promptly had me admitted for overnight observation.

It was to be one of the longest nights of my life. When the pain became too much, I would ask for more morphine, but after a few doses, they told me I had reached the maximum and they were not allowed to give me any more. I learned then just how instantly addictive morphine can be, especially when it's the only way of relieving high levels of pain.

I was climbing the walls, or at least I would have if I could have used my legs. The hours dragged until the surgeon finally appeared the next day, by which time my right calf was twice the circumference it had been the night before. I was immediately transferred to a private clinic where he could carry out a procedure to reduce the pressure that was building inside my leg.

Picture this: I am on a hospital trolley. My feet have passed through the swinging doors of an operating theatre, my torso has yet to enter. At my side is an anaesthetist. He holds a clipboard. He hands it to me and points to where I should sign. I read the document down to where my signature was meant to be.

'I'm not signing *that*!' I say.

'Why not?' he asks.

'Because you are going to take my leg off . . . I'm not signing for you to take my leg off'.

'If you don't sign, you're going to lose it anyway. We're going in there to do our best to try to save it'.

What a decision! I had no one, other than him, a nurse and a porter to advise me. No family, no friends, no one. I was not so much *in The Lonely Seat* as *on the Lonely Bed*!

'I have no choice, do I?'

'No. The blood supply to your foot is cut off. Gangrene can set in really quickly in these circumstances, and it's already been 24 hours'.

The thought hit me that if I hadn't spoken about private healthcare, my leg would have been encased in plaster as it swelled up. Valuable hours would have been lost, and as a result, so would my leg. I signed.

That episode is the only time in my life when I have availed myself of private healthcare. I've had many other episodes over the years where the British National Health Service has been nothing short of wonderful. This was just one of those strokes of good luck. I just happened to get to see the right person at the right time.

I woke up on October 18, 1980. My twenty-fifth birthday. I gingerly lifted the sheet covering my body, praying *'Please, God, let my leg be there'.* It was.

I had never been in hospital, and a super-fit twenty-five-year-old with an active mind found it very hard to adapt to being an invalid, but I didn't exactly have a choice. If I wasn't in bed, then I had to be wheeled everywhere. It wasn't long before I broke down in tears. All of my independence, that gift so important to me, was gone. I'd had just a couple of weeks of being in a wheelchair, but I knew I was going to recover. How people who are told they will never walk again cope with such things I will never know. My respect for them runs deep and comes from only having had the briefest glimpse of what they must go through.

If the pain of my being crushed was bad, there was more to come. I learned later that my injury was something known as *acute compartment syndrome.* The surgical operation to save my leg was called a *fasciotomy.* In simple terms, that meant that my lower leg was cut open, the accumulated detritus within the muscles was removed and then the wound was left open for several days. If all went well, the open wound would later be covered by skin grafted from my thigh.

After a few days I was eventually wheeled back into the theatre to have the grafts put into place. After that it was a case of waiting yet more days before I was to be taken back to the theatre to see if the grafts had been successful, which was, I was informed, by no means certain.

Apparently, the procedure was supposed to be done under general anaesthetic. I learned later that doing it that way did not suit the surgeon's busy schedule, so he decided that whilst it would still be done in a sterile operating theatre, it would take place while I was awake. The dressings around the two large wounds in my leg were removed, and the surgeon, declaring that he was pleased with the outcome, then proceeded to remove the stitches.

There was, and still is, no feeling in the grafted skin, but the normal skin around the edges was super sensitive. I yelped as, one by one, the stitches were removed. Right then I thought I understood why I should have been under anaesthetic whilst the procedure took place. Boy, I was wrong!

Because then he got to the next part: the donor site on my right thigh from where my skin had been taken. We hear of burn victims having to face months of painful skin grafts in order to recover. Well, here's the news: it's not where they put the skin, it's where they *take* it from that causes the pain. In my case, skin around the size of an exercise book had been removed from my thigh.

After the skin had been removed, the area left behind was covered with a waxy gauze. A few days later, with the bandages removed, the surgeon looked down at the gooey mass of wax and gauze and skin growing back through it. I looked down at the gooey mass too. Then, to my amazement, he began to peel it away. Think of a super-sticky sticking plaster being removed from your most sensitive place, then multiply that pain by 1,000.

The searing pain was incredible, in a way surpassing that which I had gone through when being crushed by the steel, except this time it came in waves as, millimetre by millimetre, he pulled it away. My newly grown skin was being taken with it. Apart from my screams, and yes, they were screams, the room was silent. Every nurse was concentrating on holding me down. I remember thinking: *I am being skinned alive.*

Finally, it was over.

'Well done', he said, 'you have just had the male equivalent of having a baby'.

First, how the hell would he know and, second, I wasn't in the mood for jokes. I had fallen into shock. Apparently, in my delirium, I heard the nurses saying that the procedure should never have taken place without anaesthetic. The skinning procedure took place another three or four times, each time slightly less painful than before. But the fear that I went through in anticipation of each procedure remains vivid to this day. Should I have sued him for malpractice? Maybe, but thanks to him, I still had two legs, and that was all that mattered.

After sixteen days in hospital, I was sent home to recover. I had to learn to use crutches, and with a broken right leg and a broken left foot, getting around was a bit of a challenge. Nonetheless, my car was an automatic, and after a week or so, I decided that I could drive it perfectly well. My wife could keep me at home no longer. Gary from the factory next door had helped a huge amount in my absence, making sure that my staff had some work to do. I will be forever grateful for that.

JUST WHEN YOU THINK THINGS CAN'T GET WORSE . . .

While I was in hospital, the steel that had fallen onto my legs was processed and delivered to my biggest customer. On what may well have been my first day back, the phone rang. It took me a while to reach it, as I was on crutches and it was still in the toilet! The caller told me that the company that had bought the steel had gone bust. The steel that had almost cost me my leg was not going to be paid for. That phone call wiped out everything I had in the business, almost to the penny. Receiving news like that is a bit like seeing your lottery numbers come up, only to realise that you hadn't bought a ticket that week. My rug was well and truly pulled from under me. I was all for giving up. It was my wife's words that kept me going. She only said it once, but once was enough:

'You've worked so hard and overcome so much; don't give up now'.

So, I didn't.

I know that sounds overly simple, but that's exactly the way it happened. My wife's comments were just enough to tip the balance towards me carrying on and not giving up. I called my suppliers and was honest with them about my dilemma. Their forbearance helped me survive. I can't help thinking that if I had tried to lie my way out of the situation, it would have been a different story. I don't tell lies. I never could.

Over the next year I worked twice as hard to get back on my feet, both financially and literally.

REFLECTION

What lessons did I draw from that period in my life? In all honesty, none at the time. If I'd known at the outset what would happen, I'm not so sure I would have done anything differently. The accident was just that: an accident. Could it have been avoided? Yes of course it could. It is only with hindsight that I realise that the accident, and what happened afterwards, held within it a gift. I was so close to defeat both physically and financially, and yet I wasn't defeated. As we know already, defeat only happens when we give up, and that was the lesson that served me above all else, in the decades to come.

Given what you have just read, let me ask you a few questions...

1. What would happen to your business if you weren't there? Would it still be able to operate successfully? Would your suppliers still be paid? Would your customers stay with you?

2. Just how well do you know your customers? Are there any red flags you are choosing to ignore? Don't just say 'no' to that question off the bat. Give yourself time to think about it. Be honest! And don't forget that honesty with ourselves is one of the most important traits of all. If we are not honest with ourselves, then it follows that we're kidding ourselves. And if we're kidding ourselves, then we won't see that tidal wave that is building up and about to crash over our heads.

3. Where are the physical dangers? Have you done every-thing you can to prevent them? And I don't mean just having done a risk assessment months or even years ago. Everything changes. Machines become ever-more powerful; different staff with different experience interpret danger in different ways, or don't appreci-ate it at all. Reactive is not good enough; proactive is the only way to go.

6

Get a Grip

With all that had happened since I started out, who would blame me if I'd believed that someone was sabotaging my every move? Maybe it was a good thing that such thoughts never dawned on me; otherwise I might have treated everyone I met with suspicion. You cannot go through life like that, and you certainly can't grow a business that way. You have to trust. If not, you may as well find a cave and set up in business as a hermit. Interaction is what business is about; some would argue it's what life itself is about.

The thing is, all of those setbacks helped me to create something worth having. Whoever said 'If it doesn't kill you, it will make you stronger' was absolutely correct. If my road had been a smooth one, I would not have been nearly so capable of handling what was to come in the future. I didn't have to seek out a book on developing resilience. I'd had to live it, breathe it and 'suck it up' to survive. Besides, in those days I didn't know that books on resilience existed.

Every rock strewn across my path came with a choice. I could go over it, around it or under it, or give up and retreat. Remember: we only lose when we give in, right? When we view those rocks in hindsight, they are no longer rocks that block our path but stepping stones that serve to carry us forwards, stronger and fitter than ever.

Think of building a business as climbing a mountain. If the way is strewn with rocks, then our upward progress will be a lot slower than if it is well paved. But every one of those rocks, once conquered, provides a secure foothold from which to tackle the next obstacle. If our path has been nothing but smooth, we are ill-equipped to stay on the mountain should a storm hit or the way become too steep. Our slide to the bottom as soon as things go wrong will be spectacularly fast. Anyway, by my way of thinking, it's the rocks in the road that make the journey worthwhile.

HAVING FAITH

After a few months, the company was back on an even keel and doing OK, but I still wanted more. I couldn't resist buying a newer, faster machine that had the potential to transform the business. Buying it was a huge risk. I didn't have the money to pay for it and certainly wouldn't be able to make the payments if it didn't work from the get-go. But I had unshakeable faith that the project would be a success.

Not faith in the religious sense, but faith in the fact that things would work out for the best. For much of my career, having that kind of faith became a recurring theme which has, strange as it may seem, always led to success.

The new machine didn't have the width capacity of the old one, but it was exactly nine times faster. However, it needed compressed air to operate, and I had spent all my cash on the down payment for it. Fortune smiled on me when Gary, my kindly next-door neighbour, once again came to my aid and allowed me to run a line from his compressor into my building. However, his compressor was on the opposite side of the factory.

There was no chance of simply trailing a pneumatic hose across the floor. It would have to be 'flown', passing it through the eaves of the roof some thirty or forty feet above. I had learned many skills in my few short months in business. By now, welding, basic electrics, machinery removals and installation were all on my CV. Now it was time to learn a new skill: climbing up into the rafters of a roof and crawling across the narrow beam of an overhead crane with no safety net or harness. As a youngster I had loved climbing trees; it was all great fun. But this was different. Now I was an adult with a bad leg, a healthy dose of fear and no money to pay someone else to do it. I gingerly threaded the nylon hose across the roof space, making my way slowly, inch by inch, from one side to the other.

I had used a ladder to climb up, and now it had been moved and waited for me to descend on the other side. It was time to leave my perch, let go of the steelwork and step onto the ladder. I tried to do just that, but nothing happened. Try as I might, I couldn't persuade my hands to let go of the roof's steelwork. Gary's sales manager, Terry, stood at the bottom of the ladder calling encouragement. It wasn't working. As it happened, Terry's hobby was rock climbing. He spotted my dilemma as something that happens to rock climbing newbies.

'You've gripped up', he called.

'What's that supposed to mean?' asked a shaky voice high above him.

He explained that what I was going through was very common, and that the way to overcome it was to be talked down, move by move. After what seemed like an age, his explanation finally helped me understand what was happening and, within minutes, he had me moving my left leg a few inches to the left and six inches down, and then my right hand to the steel beam just to my right. Stage by stage, I made it back to the ground, poignantly only a couple of feet away from where I had been crushed a few months previously. It could have ended so differently; but for Terry, I might still have been up there to this day.

That episode will probably not be the only one within these pages where I make myself look something of a fool. I guess I've never been particularly scared of that. I was always the kid in the classroom who dared to put up his hand to ask the question that everyone else in the class was too scared to ask. So, why would I include the story here? Is there some kind of a lesson to be learnt? You bet there is.

When we are in fear, nothing works properly. Our mind goes into self-preservation mode. Stuck up in that roof, nothing I told myself was making any sense. Moving one hand slightly to a safe grip was perfectly logical, but not to me. My brain was incapable of processing that instruction of its own accord. It took quite a few minutes, but I had to learn to trust someone else's judgement in order to let go and move one tiny stage at a time. Once I was on the ground, what I'd just gone through was laughable. But know this: **when fear or stress walks through the door, the ability to make sensible decisions jumps out the window.**

REFLECTION

No matter who we are or what we do, we all experience times of stress, and stress is just another form of fear. It is the fear that our abilities aren't adequate to solve the problems we are facing in the time we have available. How often do we wish there was someone around who could share the burden, someone who has travelled this road before, someone who can talk us through our situation, move by move, maybe inch by inch until we reach solid ground? At that moment, we might see that person as some kind of angel, helping us reset the chess pieces of our life. But what's in it for them? Why the heck should they give up their time and energy to help?

Let me answer that with a short story. Picture this.

It is a dreadful day. A relentless wind is driving the freezing rain so that it is almost horizontal. A man is standing, forlorn, next to his broken-down car. He was on his way to a business meeting, which is his last chance to earn enough commission to stop the bank from taking away his house, which they have been threatening to do for months. He has not a penny to his name to pay for a breakdown service. His mobile phone gave up last month, and he hasn't been able to find the money to replace it. He has no one to turn to. He is in The Lonely Seat. How do I know what he feels like? Because that person could easily have been me on more than one occasion.

Now picture a thirty-something CEO. He is speeding down that same road in his expensive car. Speeding because he thinks he and his car are above the rules; rules are meant for others. He's on his way to the next deal, which will make him yet another fortune. He hasn't seen his wife and kids for a while, but he's sure they're OK — they have everything they need, everything money can buy. His arrogance knows no bounds, and why should it? He's *made it*: he's the man! How do I know what he is feeling? Because basically, I have just described myself at some point in my life.

But here's the thing: if he only knew that by pulling to the side of the road and getting out of his car to offer to help that poor guy, he would have the BEST day he can remember. That's what acts of kindness can do. And that is what "The Lonely Seat" is all about.

7

Through Thick and Thin

It was happening quite often that the steel we had in stock wasn't quite the right thickness to match the orders we had on hand. Phoning around in a sellers' market to try to locate steel of the correct thickness was not my idea of fun and usually ended up with us having to pay over the odds. I realised that if I could find a machine that could squeeze steel down to a different thickness by re-rolling it, not only would we need to carry less stock, we would also be much better able to react to orders as they came in.

Fortune smiled on me yet again, and within a few days of deciding to buy one, I had found an ancient but very much over-engineered rolling mill to do the job. Now, I won't go into the technical niceties of steel rolling mills, but once again my faith had kicked in, and I had no doubt I was doing the right thing and that the rolling mill I'd chosen would do a good job. However, it didn't do a good job: it did a great job! With the help of someone who became a huge friend to me, called Harold Evans, whom I dragged out of retirement because of his technical expertise, I became a cold-rolled steel strip manufacturer, which sounded far grander than just 'steel stockholder'.

THE ROAD TO SUCCESS IS PAVED WITH ZINC

The kind of steel I dealt in came in several forms, often coated with aluminium or, more commonly zinc, which had been applied using a hot-dipped or electrolytic galvanizing process. On one occasion, we had taken on an order to supply some galvanized steel, which I could not fulfil because the parent material was slightly too thick. I took a chance and passed it through my rolling mill to reduce its thickness by just a tiny fraction of a millimetre. It worked! I began to do it more and more often.

Perhaps others had done the same in the past. However, I have always claimed that creativity and imagination are my strongest traits, and I saw huge potential in what we had done. The point of using cold-rolled steel strip is to achieve close tolerances in the material thicknesses and a specific hardness so that the product will have the correct structural integrity and strength.

After the product has been made, it can be sent for galvanizing or zinc plating, both very expensive processes when done component by component. It occurred to me that if I could roll already galvanized steel to achieve the hardness tolerances clients wanted, it would save them a huge amount of money in galvanizing costs. What I was doing was, in effect, 'bi-metal rolling', and any physics teacher will tell you that when two different metals are attached to each other and heat is applied (which is what happens when metal is passed through a rolling mill), they will expand at different rates, causing the combined metal to buckle.

In those days, the major player in the UK steel industry was the British Steel Corporation. Their technical experts declared that what I was doing was impossible. But we were doing it. Yes, it took a fair bit of trial and error to learn how, and a fair degree of testing to find out what happened to the thickness of the zinc coating, but we managed it.

Of course, a lot of clients pooh-poohed the idea, but many more embraced the concept and saved themselves a fortune. I can't claim that it was my invention, but I do claim that I was the first to spot its potential. In later years, rivals did it better and faster than me, but I did pretty well out of it too.

REFLECTION

Einstein said that everything we see was once imagined. We can go religious and include the earth and the stars in that contention, or we can stay much closer to home with industry, where every man-made object had to be first imagined before it could come into existence.

So many businesses lose sight of the value of imagination. Whether you are a student or a startup, a janitor or a boss, the finest capital you have is your imagination. Feed it, don't starve it and hide it away.

Oh, and just one more thing. I mentioned earlier in this chapter that the rolling mill I bought was over-engineered. That machine was old and clunky, but it never missed a beat. Take time to over-engineer anything you build, be it a machine, a business or yourself. It's a great way to create the resilience that one day you will surely need.

8

How Hard Can It Be?

Cold rolling steel is a bit of an art form. In simple terms, steel is passed through a pair of rollers and comes out of the other side thinner, longer, hotter (you would get hot if you were squeezed through a mangle) and harder. Without going to an outside laboratory, there was no way of measuring the hardness of the steel we produced. I needed a testing machine of my own, which meant somehow finding yet more money that I didn't have.

My work director's brother was himself a director of a well-established steel business. He and his partners were planning to close down their business and retire, so there was a good chance they might sell me their testing machine at a reasonable price. I went along to see the machine and, before I left, I had agreed to purchase the whole company, lock, stock and barrel. I had no idea how I was going to pay for it, but once again my 'having faith' button kicked in, and I was certain that it would work out.

It took about a month to complete the deal and, as it happened, our companies shared the same accountant, who acted as an honest broker between us. We sat in his office and went through how and when I would pay them. My only worry was what value they had put on their stock. I was sure that they would probably want more for it than I was prepared or even able to pay. Then I got the shock of my life, though I dared not show it.

In their mind, the price I was paying INCLUDED the stock. I had thought I would have to pay for it separately. As I saw it, there was more value in the stock than in the rest of the deal put together. Having signed and sealed the agreement, I drove back to my office, banging on the steering wheel of my car in absolute glee. I had made it: I'd done my first takeover with absolutely no money of my own. I had effectively bought a company using its own money. This was in 1985, and as far as I know, before anyone had written a book on the subject. The company had money in the bank plus a big enough overdraft facility to pay for itself. Or so I thought!

We had just about got everything up and running when I received a phone call. It was from my bank manager who happened to also be the bank manager for the company I had just purchased. He asked me to pay him a visit.

'Seems like you've done a sweet deal', he said when I sat in front of him a couple of days later. Then he hit me between the eyes. 'The thing is, Keith, your overdraft and their overdraft ...'

He paused.

'What about them?' I asked.

'I think you have relied on being able to use them both in order to get your deal over the line', he said. 'There's nothing wrong with that, but I can't let you add them together. I'm afraid I have to withdraw one or the other overdraft facility'.

WOOOSH! That was the sound of the wind coming out of my sails. Suddenly, the cash resources I had to run my business had been cut in half. At best, it was going to take some juggling. At worst, it could finish us if it meant that we couldn't pay our suppliers on time.

But so long as we don't panic, we can still think straight, make sensible decisions and, most importantly, get creative. Much of my subsequent survival, once again, came down to being honest. Both of my companies were buying from the same set of suppliers, and by that time I'd built up a good reputation with them. It turned out that they were fine with giving me extended credit while I brought things back onto an even keel. As it happened, the cash flow storm on the horizon was nowhere near as bad as I'd feared as I left the bank manager's office.

Firstly, the extra stock that I'd inherited meant that I hadn't had to buy nearly so much to meet our sales orders, so there was far less to pay out over the next couple of months. Secondly, now there were two lots of sales going out of the door with only one set of overheads. Within a year, we had established a reputation for paying early. A rare thing indeed in the steel industry.

To say we were doing well was an understatement. And yet, I didn't notice. I had moved both businesses under one roof. Visitors would laugh at our ramshackle factory — it was even featured on TV as an example of industrial decline in the Black Country — but I didn't care. By then, all that mattered to me, and I mean ALL that mattered to me, was the money I was making!

REFLECTION

Alarm bells were probably ringing, but I was refusing to hear them. I saw my happiness as being based on money: the more I had, the happier I would be. Nothing else mattered.

Decades would pass before I realised how wrong I was. Decades before I realised that my happiness didn't lie at the end of a financial rainbow. How many times have we heard *money is the root of all evil*, and *a fool and his money are soon parted* (that's one I can certainly identify with). But the years have given me a quote of my own:

Money is just do-good tokens. If you don't do good with it, what's the point of having it?

9

Be Nice (Part 1)

My sister came to work for me. Her banking background made her a great asset, and she relieved me of a significant part of my workload by taking over accounting and credit control. My own bookkeeping now consisted of a handwritten record of despatches. It was my bible, telling me what had gone out of the door, who had bought it and how much profit we had made out of it. It told me where we were in terms of profit and performance, and if you know where you are, you know where you're going.

Though I didn't see it at the time, money had become an obsession. All I cared about was getting more and more of it. Nothing else mattered. My sister was pretty brave when she tentatively asked: 'Keith, why don't you stop to smell the roses?'

My reply speaks volumes as to the kind of person I had become:

'What f****** roses?'

Yet somewhere inside, the nice version of Keith still existed.

When I first did my takeover deal, as I said, the new company's works director and my own work director were brothers.

They had another brother who worked as a maintenance and development engineer and occasional truck driver in the newly acquired company. Harold, my works director, had taken me to one side when the takeover was being negotiated: 'You will need to let him go, Keith. Let him retire as part of the package. I know he's my brother, but he's a bolshy so-and-so; he will never work for *you*'.

'We'll see', I smiled, paying more heed to my faith that things would work out than to his worries.

His brother's name was Jim. I soon learned that he said what was on his mind, but then again, so did I. Both of us were always dead straight with each other, and he continued to work for me after he retired, even through the dark times that were to hit us a few years later. Frankly, I don't know what I would have done without him and the irreplaceable skills he possessed.

His favourite reading, he once told me, consisted of books that recounted how engineering feats such as bridge building were accomplished against all the odds. As an engineer, there seemed to be nothing he couldn't do. When he drove the company truck, he was impeccable and totally reliable.

His driving days came to an end when, on a trip to Manchester, he suffered what turned out to be a mild heart attack. He suspected he knew it had happened but foolishly chose to drive the truck back to the factory before taking himself to hospital so that I wouldn't have the problem of trying to collect it. In fairness though, he also later admitted that he didn't fancy being in hospital a hundred miles away from home.

Both of his brothers were amazed at the relationship we developed, yet once we got to know each other, neither Jim nor I shared that surprise. I learned a huge amount about managing people thanks to him. I liked him. Give people a chance to shine and they will surprise you; respect them for what they can do, and take heed of what they tell you, especially if it's clear that they know more than you. Most of all, *genuinely* care about them. Chances are they will care back.

WHEN THE BRAIN NEEDS TO PLAY CATCH-UP

There is one more thing that I want to talk about before this particular episode draws to a close. It happened from the moment I had bought the second company and lasted several months. I was totally unprepared for it, and I suspect that so is anyone else who takes over a business or the boss's chair for the first time. What shocked me was the fact that suddenly, apart from rent, I had two sets of everything to deal with. Two sales ledgers, two lots of production machines, two sets of employees who had to learn how to live with each other. And it all sat at my door. I had suddenly placed a huge call on my intellectual ability, my brain power.

I was being pushed and pulled from pillar to post in ways that I never expected. Gradually, a bit like a muscle growing steadily stronger when it is put under stress, my brain power caught up. But it was a warning; it could have so easily gone the other way. If you are about to take over another business, or start up at a second location, brace yourself for a rough ride in the early days, and try to get someone around you who can help you carry the load. Bear in mind, they may well be working for your target company and just desperate to show what they can do, so don't just look at the numbers, look at the people before you sign on the dotted line.

REFLECTION

Those around you might help you, but they cannot hope to understand. Chances are it will be too late to reach out to those who have trodden your path before. But if we have already nurtured that group of people, already have the kind of non-judgemental friends we might turn to, then our path can be so much smoother.

Ask yourself these questions:

1. Who have you got in your circle of friends who you can be certain would take your call when you need an arm put around you?

2. Who have you got in your circle of friends who knows instinctively that you would be there for them if the circumstances were reversed?

10

No Money Down ... Almost

The 1980s were merging into the 1990s. We were doing well. I was taking regular holidays and always joked that my staff could tell just how good my holiday had been by how bad a mood I was in when I returned to work. Though, I suspect they didn't necessarily see the funny side of it. The thing is, I can see now that the success was starting to change me; money was becoming more and more important. I guess it had become something of a drug.

I had rearranged the working week so that by starting an hour early and taking no lunch, everyone could finish early on Fridays. I might claim that that was to give my staff more freedom and a better way of working, but truth be told I had changed the Friday hours for my own ends. I wanted everything, and that included an aeroplane. Friday afternoons had become my time to take flying lessons. The problem was that work was starting to take over my life. Apart from holidays, I had little time for anything else. Increasingly, I found I couldn't get away from work on time. I'd have to drive like a maniac to make it to the airfield on time. Stupid!

I had known a few millionaires before I started out, and the one thing I noticed was that none of them were particularly happy, certainly no happier than me. I wanted to be the first *happy* millionaire I knew. I didn't realise it then, but while I might have been on the way to being a millionaire, I was certainly not on the road to happiness. I was on a hamster wheel of my own making. Nothing I had was enough; it was all about getting more.

BUY WHEN NOBODY ELSE WANTS TO

Throughout my career I've always been something that I call a *counter-cyclical expansionist*: for me, when times are bad, that's the time to expand. I had built a decent business during the recession of the 1980s and now, as the '90s arrived, industry was finding it tough. A large steel company was divesting itself of a machine which, if I could get my hands on it, would mean a quantum leap for my business. In football terms, it would have taken us from Division Three to Division One and allowed us to play with the big boys.

The problem was that there was no way on God's good earth we would be able to shoehorn it into our premises. Its footprint would have taken up the whole of the factory floor. But the price was too good to miss. Even though I had nowhere to put it, I bought it anyway, paying for storage until I could find a suitable factory to accommodate it . . . yet another episode of me having faith. I paid a sizeable chunk of money up front and put the rest on hire purchase. That's the advantage of having a good credit rating. The monthly payments would have been crippling if we weren't doing well, but we were, and like I said, I had faith.

In the light of my (in my mind) unstoppable expansion, friends began to ask if I would employ them. One in particular, Dave, was an excellent salesman who wasn't happy where he was. He and I had been good friends for several years, and it was a no-brainer; he was the man! With his arrival I knew we were going to have to redouble our efforts to find premises big enough to house the new machine, but it wasn't easy, particularly because I refused to rent. I wanted to buy, even though at the time I was down to more or less zero in the bank. Dave's arrival should have meant that the company turnover went up, and with it the profitability, but it didn't work out that way. It wasn't his fault; it was mine because I hadn't thought it through. Dave's customer base was different to mine. He sold more tonnage than I did, but at significantly lower margins. But even after saying that, the margins weren't the problem. It was much more to do with the fact that in order to service his customers, I was having to put my existing clients to the back of the queue. Turnover was up, but profitability was down. I needed a new factory . . . fast!

I found myself looking at several candidates and made an offer on one, only to have it rejected in favour of a lower one because I didn't want to take it over for another two months. By that time, I was sure I would have found the deposit. Yet another episode of me having faith.

ANYONE FOR TENNIS?

Even though I was looking for something around 16,000 to 25,000 square feet, I couldn't help noticing that there was a substantially larger factory just around the corner. The fact that it was over 90,000 square feet didn't bother me; I could sublet what I didn't need. It had belonged to a manufacturer of giant presses, the kind that make body panels for cars, and as such it had heavy overhead cranes and deep pits sunk into its concrete floor. It was absolutely ideal for what I wanted.

I contacted the agent and was given the Royal Tour. The whole place needed some work, but I'd seen much worse. The offices, however, presented a bit more of a dilemma. They were, shall we say, somewhat too large for my needs, but to my mind, there was nothing to stop me from subletting them. Then they took me to see what, back in the day, had been the epicentre of the company's innovation over the last half century. It was their drawing and design office. It was the size of a tennis court. The glass roof designed to maximise the light was leaking badly.

I had no idea what I would do with it. It was in no state to be sublet. Nevertheless, the place as a whole had my ambition bone twitching. If I remember correctly, it was up for sale for around nine hundred thousand pounds. I think I offered six hundred and fifty thousand, and to my surprise they said yes. I would have had to find the deposit, but the bank had already said they would finance the rest. It was a classic case of the time to buy is when everyone else wants to sell. But then I got cold feet.

It was not the prospect of finding the deposit, although at the time I didn't know where I would get it, nor was it the prospect of having to find tenants. It was that bloody drawing office! My creativity bone had come up short. I had no idea of what I would do with it short of spending two hundred thousand pounds to knock it down and build something else in its place. And since I would have been severely lacking in cash if I had taken on the deal, that wasn't ever going to be an option. It was one of those occasions when I did not have faith.

No one knew that I'd put in an offer which had been accepted. No one was whispering not to do it in my ear. It was my own gut feeling that this would be a step too far.

Time went on, and I was still looking. Truth is, I couldn't justify Dave, my new sales director, nor could I afford to keep Andy, the new production manager I had taken on at the same time. Their efforts and contributions were being strangled by the company's inability to process enough material. But I knew that in the long term I needed them. Once we had found new premises and deployed the new machinery, they would be in their element.

Times were not good in the steel industry at that time. Another stockholder had bought a whole factory estate, and the downturn had left him short of cash. He asked if I would like to take a look at a 20,000 square foot factory. It wasn't much more than a tin hut, but it had cranage. Problem was, its cranes would only lift a couple of tonnes. I wanted to lift steel coils that weighed anything up to twenty tonnes! Besides, by now I didn't have the deposit. Cash was still on a downward slide. Then my creative bone kicked in.

This was in the days before anyone wrote books about doing property deals with no money down, and in fairness, I think when they did get around to writing them, they weren't thinking of the kind of deal I had in mind. I realised that the one thing I had was a good credit rating with the machinery finance company. I could leverage that fact. This is the deal I offered to the factory owner.

'I will give you the price you ask, but I want to buy the cranes separately', I said.

He agreed, telling me that he didn't care how the deal was structured, so long as he was paid.

As far as I was concerned, I had bought three cranes and a factory. My ownership of the cranes served as a deposit. In buying the cranes separately, that represented the 15 percent deposit for the factory I needed. After the deal was done, I refinanced the cranes for a 10 percent deposit on their value. This meant that I had purchased the factory with just a 1.5 percent deposit.

I admit that this deal would never have worked if the property hadn't been well below its market value, and I'm not sure how legal that kind of thing is nowadays, but the mortgage was paid, and the crane hire purchase was paid off, so everyone was a winner.

REFLECTION

There is one attribute that perhaps above all others has to run alongside imagination through an entrepreneur's veins: you have to have balls. I don't mean balls in the literal sense; I have met many ladies who have balls to spare. I mean, the kind of balls that allow you to be audacious. Believe me, that's where success by whatever measure you want to use is to be found.

11

Holes Cost Money

It took several long and frustrating weeks before I could begin to move the new machinery out of storage. Now it was time to build the foundations needed to install it, and that involved a whole new venture into the wonderful world of civil engineering in the form of laying the foundations for by far the biggest machine I had ever installed.

Every component was on a different level. Some were to sit on concrete plinths; others would stand on the floor but required really deep and substantial foundations beneath them. We dug holes where we needed them and built 'shuttering' around where the plinths were to go. For those of you who don't know what shuttering is, it's usually fabricated from plywood that is fixed in place so as to act as a mould for wet concrete to be poured. When the concrete has set, the shuttering is removed, and you have a concrete plinth. On this occasion, the shuttering operation took the best part of a week.

Truckloads of mixed concrete turned up. We filled the holes that needed filling, and by afternoon we were ready to start the biggest part of the project: the plinths. All was going well until with a sudden creak, part of the shuttering gave way. Tonnes of wet concrete poured out. We shovelled and swore in equal proportion, trying to stem the tide. We had to delay the last few truckloads of concrete but managed to get the shuttering back into some kind of position so that we could carry on.

The end result was a shape that was somewhat artistic in its interpretation of what had been originally intended. By the time the project was completed, we had poured two hundred and fifty tonnes of concrete. It didn't look that good, but it did the job. It was one of those occasions when no matter their job title or status, everyone mucked in. That's a sign of a good team, one that we should keep together, because they *pull together*. I must have done something in the past to deserve them.

Next, we needed to dig a bloody big hole. Such things are known in the industry as looping pits. They give the steel somewhere to go as it transits through the machine instead of all over the floor.

A concrete-lined hole is incredibly expensive to create, especially when it's as big and deep as the one I wanted. There was no way we were going to pay twenty or thirty thousand pounds to have one put in. Creativity was called for. One of my companies (I had a few by then) employed a machine operator who happened to be a skilled steel fabricator. I had him build a tank which we could then stand on its end, using our newly installed 25-tonne crane, before lowering it into an oversized hole dug by the deepest capacity excavator I could hire.

Then we could simply pour concrete around it, right? Wrong! I had the tank made to 25 feet long because that was the height under the crane. What I forgot was that, before it could be set upright, it would have to pass through the diagonal, which mathematicians amongst you will understand was getting on for 27 feet.

There I was with a dirty great hole half full of water (we had found the water table at just 10 feet below ground level) and a tank sitting next to it which was going nowhere. After a great deal of head scratching, we managed to prop up the tank at a precarious angle, then used the crane from some distance away to drag it upright. I suspect that the process may well have fallen foul of the factory inspector, but in my defence, as was always the case, if anyone was going to be in danger, it was me.

Plop! In it went. Concrete was poured around it and allowed to set. I knew that we wouldn't have a problem with the water leaking in because we had built a fully welded tank. Wrong again. We had our own swimming pool. From then on, there was always a sizeable puddle outside the factory when a pump had been turned on to get rid of the nightly accumulation of water.

The story of the hole didn't quite end there. Shortly after it had been installed, I received a mysterious call from some-one. All he said was:

'I've heard you've just taken on a new factory'.

'Yes', said I, slightly suspiciously.

'Would you be interested in renting it to us for 24 hours?'

'Why?' I asked, very much more suspiciously.

'We'd like to hold a rave in there. You've got plenty of space, and there are no houses nearby'.

'I don't think so, mate'.

'We will pay you'.

'No, mate. No thanks'.

'How does sixty thousand pounds sound?'

You could hear my temptation bell ringing from a mile away. But then the sound of prison doors clanging rang even louder.

'No, mate, there's a dirty great pit in the middle of the factory. They'd throw away the key if anyone fell down there'.

That pit had cost me sixty thousand pounds. Mind you, I don't think I would ever have allowed it anyway. I suspect that the money made by these particular promoters might not have necessarily relied on what they charged on the door. The prison doors would have stayed closed for a very long time. Nevertheless, it was an interesting money-making concept, but as they say . . . if you can't do the time, don't do the crime.

REFLECTION

Business is all about risk. It's about weighing up the size of the prize against the consequences of failure. Whilst I didn't want to fail, I accepted that it was a possibility. Nevertheless, I felt that if I kept control of the game, then unlike betting on the horses, I could stack the odds in my favour. That's still as true now as it was all those years ago. For me, the prospect of going to jail if something failed was a step too far. But then, circumstances had not pushed me into a corner.

As I've said before, when stress walks through the door, the ability to make sensible decisions jumps out the window. There are many examples of business owners going to jail after turning to crime to bail out their business, and there are countless instances of those who have done so who got away with it. When someone has lived and breathed their business year after year, they will almost sell their children rather than lose it.

12

Don't Poke Your Screwdriver Where It's Not Welcome

The new factory was four miles away from my old one, and for six months I operated both. I had two sets of staff throwing questions at me from two different sites. My life was such that I might just as well have pitched a tent midway between them. Why was it that my staff didn't seem to be able to handle problems?

Hindsight now tells me that it was all my fault. For too long I had kept everything to myself. Because I could handle things, I hadn't trained anyone else to do it in my absence. I was such a hypocrite. I so often told my managers that a good manager is one who trains those in their team so well that they themselves are no longer needed.

I have seen managers make sure that those on their team can never be as good as them by inadequate training or leaving their staff out of key conversations. As someone who has employed quite a few people in my time, I will say this: the manager who clearly teaches the senior member of a team to such a level that they could do the job as well as themselves and encourages them to help their own subordinates in the same way is the one who should be least in fear of losing their job. Indeed, they should find themselves at the head of the queue when there is a promotion in the air.

That is, at least, how it *should* be, but all too often we find organisations with toxic environments where everyone is in fear of losing their job. Bosses who promote that toxicity, whether by accident or design, do not realise that in the long run it is *they* who are the losers. They are signing the death warrant for the business as they lead it into steady decline. When they want to retire, there will be no one from their ranks who can take over. Their only option will be to sell the business for a far lower figure than they might have or stay for years and years while the new owners try to find a replacement for them. All of this from the short-sightedness of not allowing people to grow to their potential.

Anyway, back to my story. I was on a giant piece of elastic stretching the four miles between my two factories. On one occasion, I had left my new factory and had barely reached the front door of my older one when I was called back:

'Keith, all the electrics have gone off on the new machine'.

Back I went. I crawled on my hands and knees under the stationary machine to the electrical panel. I didn't bother turning off the power; I would be fine — I had an insulated screwdriver. Wrong again! Whilst it did stop me getting much of a shock, my reliance on its insulation made me far too cocky. As I poked and prodded, there was a bright white flash and an explosion that threw me backwards.

Shit! I was blind! I reversed myself back from the panel under the machine to my waiting staff on my hands and knees. All I could see was blackness. I felt a kind of stoic resignation that I'd done something really stupid and that I was going to have to pay for it for the rest of my life.

Gradually (thank heavens) my eyesight began to return. After an hour, I could see well enough to drive back to my office, but wiser heads told me that I should go to hospital as I had likely suffered something called a 'welding flash'. The hospital confirmed that I had burned both eyes and warned me that they would become very uncomfortable for the next few days.

In saying that, they won that year's award for understatement. Before I got home it felt like my eyes had grains of sand in them. By midnight, the whole Sahara had relocated into my eye sockets. On a discomfort scale of one to ten, it scored about a hundred! It was days before I managed to get back to normal. Whatever that was!

REFLECTION

Why do I tell this particular story? What lessons might be drawn from it? Well, there are two, I guess. The first is that just because I happened to be the best at doing something, didn't mean that I should insist upon doing it. Someone could have done a 75 percent job, and the company would still have been better off because the boss was free to be elsewhere doing stuff that brought a greater benefit than this one. I didn't learn that lesson then, even though it almost cost me my sight.

I am not saying that it was a job I should have delegated to one of my team, heaven forbid; they weren't electricians. But I had created an environment where all problems were to be laid at the boss's door. It would be years before I finally realised how much more successful I'd have been if almost losing my eyes had made me properly open them to the fundamental mistake I was making.

And what of the second lesson? That's easy. Don't poke dangerous things. They may bite.

13

You Will Fill It with Stock!

The day we took possession of the factory, Harold, my works director, and I walked into the empty building. It seemed cavernous.

'You know you'll fill this with stock', he said.

'Not a chance', I replied.

Within three months the factory was full to the brim. How did I turn out to be so wrong?

Just a few months later the invoices for all of that extra stock were landing on my desk and were soon to become due for payment. There was no way I could pay them all on time without borrowing more money, so it was off to the bank again. This time, as I sat in my usually ever-so-helpful bank manager's office, he said no to increasing my overdraft but offered me an alternative. He could arrange for a factoring facility to be put into place.

Factoring is a mechanism whereby you borrow money against your book debts. Sell something to Mr Smith for a thousand pounds that isn't due for payment for another two months, and the bank will lend you eight hundred as soon as you raise the invoice. The bank then owns the debt, and they will chase the money when it becomes due. As soon as Mr Smith pays, the bank will send you the remaining two hundred, minus their fees.

I have never liked the idea of factoring. It can be notoriously expensive. Of the two hundred pounds still to come in from the above example, a great deal of it will likely disappear into the bank's coffers as costs, especially if Mr Smith pays late. Which brings us to my second issue — if the bank gets wind that Mr Smith is in trouble and might not pay at all, it will immediately take back the money it has advanced.

And then there is the problem that you are no longer chasing your own invoices. Picture this: Mr Smith has a thousand in the bank. He owes Mr Jones, one of your rivals, a thousand, and he owes your factors a thousand too. Clearly, he cannot pay both. Someone will have to wait. He believes that by not paying your factors, he will do less damage to you than he would do to Mr Jones if he doesn't pay him.

After all, Mr Smith's relationship is with you and Mr Jones, not with your faceless factors. If the factors resort to legal action, then he will stop ordering from you. Your factors can do nothing to enhance your relationship with Mr Smith but a great deal to endanger it. In my experience, when money is tight, factored invoices are put to the back of the queue. Another problem I had with factoring was the common perception that as soon as a company factored their accounts, they were on a downward slope.

But in hindsight I should have spotted a much more insideous reason to be wary. Factoring is great at first; suddenly you have all this extra liquidity at your disposal, and your growth is easily financed. Bigger sales mean more money, but, when there is a downturn, then cash availability follows suit . . . instantly!

Management starts to take its eye off the bottom line and places it firmly onto the sales ledger. The company starts to take on orders at any cost. Margins are eroded, goods are sold at a loss, just for the sake of gaining a sale. Poor credit ratings are not allowed to stand in the way of sales because wages are due to be paid tomorrow or maybe a supplier will stop deliveries if we don't pay them on time. Why do I know this? Because having had no choice but to accept the bank's offer to give me a factoring facility, these things happened to me.

I'd always been keen on producing cash flow forecasts and thus had spotted the need for extra finance a few weeks before we actually needed the money. This proved somewhat fortunate since what should have been a quick and easy process took several weeks to get into place.

The bank's factoring division declared they would be prepared to extend a facility to me, but only if I computerised my accounts. Why did I need a computer? Our records were impeccable. We knew, to the penny, where we were, who owed us what and what we owed to others. But they were adamant.

Several thousand pounds later I had one on my desk. From that day onwards, I had lost control of my finances. We were always playing catch-up. Yes, it gave the bank an up-to-date sales ledger, but in the early '90s, it was the computer tail wagging the company dog.

REFLECTION

There were questions I should have asked myself, not just occasionally but constantly. If it is to survive, any enterprise has to be dynamic, continuously making changes as they are needed, but better still, being proactive and planning for the changes in advance. And yes, I realise that is so much easier said than done, but it shouldn't stop us from embracing things such as SWOT analyses into our structure. For those of you who haven't heard the term, SWOT stands for Strengths, Weaknesses, Opportunities and Threats. Such things are every bit as important to a one-man band as they are to a multinational.

1. What changes are you intending to make to a new business that will make things better or easier?

2. If you introduce them, will they work straight off the bat, or will you probably have to tweak them to be fit for use in your organisation?

3. Are the changes so valuable that you are prepared to alter or discard aspects of the business that have served you so well up to now? Did you make sure that you considered the widest applications of your proposals? To what extent are you going to let the tail of change wag the organisation dog?

4. Do you know where you are? I mean exactly where you are. How is the business performing? Is profitability going in the right direction? Are sales in line with expectations? The list goes on and on, but the bottom line is this: always, always, always know where you are. Because if you don't, how can you know which direction to steer?

14

Name Your Price

Our trading brought us regularly into contact with some of the UK's steel importers. One of them was keen to establish a facility in the Midlands, and discussions took place as to the possibility of us providing the processing base they needed. I found myself increasingly confident that the work they were promising to send us would easily cover the new factory's overheads.

The day came when we were ready to press the 'go' button. Their management team came up to spend the day with us so as to satisfy themselves that we could make good on our part of the bargain. This is how the conversation went:

'We like what we see. How much do you want for it?'

'What do you mean?'

'We would like to buy you out. How much do you want?'

I told them that I didn't want to sell it, I wanted to build it. I never heard from them again.

It seemed that whatever it was that we were doing, we were getting the attention of bigger players in the market. I won't say that they were offers to buy me out, but there were several that invited me to name my price. But my answer was always the same: 'No thanks'. I was having a great time.

I have met very successful people who live by the rule that they take the first offer. The strategy has worked for them, and they are exceptionally wealthy. This has always been counter-intuitive to me, and I guess I will never change, even though looking back I know it has cost me millions. Now I know that I should not have rejected offers out of hand. I should have given them serious consideration, knowing that if I accepted them, I would be free to move on to build something else. I should have realised that the game I was in (and to me, at that point it was indeed a game) was not the only game in town.

Selling a business that we might have spent most of our lives building into something worthwhile, missing our children's sports days and family things that others take for granted, is a once-in-a-lifetime event. Chances are, if we're lucky, it will be the biggest deal we ever do, and yet . . . the opportunity to sell may come when we least expect, and usually when we don't want it, a fleeting moment that can change the rest of our lives.

A HEALTH WARNING

DISCLAIMER: Please note that the following comments regarding "Business Sales Brokers" are my personal observastions of the industry in general. They are not aimed at any particular companies.

In the world of business, indeed like most things in life, there are good guys and bad guys. The organisations who offer to sell your business for you have their share of the latter.

Picture this: you have decided to sell up and retire. One of your options is to use an agent to market it for you. You find a few likely candidates and ask them to value it. Just like real estate agents or brokers, they each want your business, and they know you want the best price, so they value it in the hope that their value is the highest. You like the sales pitch and what they promise they will achieve and decide to sign a contract with one of them. You pay a significant up-front fee, and they put you on their listing.

After a few months nothing has happened. You call them to be told, 'we have some interest, but we think you may have to reduce the price if you want a quick sale'.

Months become years, and still there has been no sale, despite your willingness to accept a lower and lower price. Three years have gone by while you may well have taken your eye off the ball. You decide to give up and take it off the market. A year later, out of the blue, a friend asks you if you would like to sell. You strike a deal, and the sale goes through. Then the invoice arrives. The sales agent has spotted the change of ownership and is claiming their percentage of the sale value. Your response that they had no part in finding the buyer meets with them pointing to the small print in the contract you signed years ago. They have done nothing illegal; frankly it is your own fault for signing the contract whilst the stars surrounding the glittering prize were in your eyes.

There is anecdotal evidence that suggests that the income generated by these agents arises not from successful sales of clients' businesses but from up-front, nonreturnable retention fees and their pursuit of clients who have sold their business separately, having not been aware that they were liable to pay a commission, which as it turns out is anything but a success fee.

REFLECTION

If you're thinking of appointing an agent to sell your business, read the small print of any contract, and refuse to sign it if it's not to your liking. Don't let some (as my mum called them) 'fine-mouthed salesman' persuade you otherwise. If they really want to sell your business, and truly believe they can, then they should be prepared to put their money where their mouth is and accept the fact that they need to change their 'standard' contract which has made them so much money in the past at the expense of unhappy clients.

15

Buying from the Right People

The processing work we had been counting on came to nothing. Not for the first time, I had put more or less all of my eggs in one basket. Now I had to get off my backside and generate some business to be able to grow into the overheads that I had taken on. One evening, the phone rang. Salespeople often choose to call at around 6:00 p.m., because they know that if it is a small business, there is a good chance that the boss will pick up the phone. This was going to be one of those calls.

The man politely introduced himself and said that in fact he was calling on behalf of his son, who had just built a stock-control software package. He'd heard that we had recently opened up and wondered if he could call around to show me how it worked. I laughed that we had only recently bought our first computer and had barely learned how to plug it in. But if he would give me a couple of months until we were settled, he would be welcome to pay me a visit.

'Thank you for being so polite', he said. 'There are many who would have just put the phone down on me. Now can I tell you the real reason for my call?'

'Go on', I said, somewhere between suspicious and intrigued.

He explained that he was the chief executive of a large tube manufacturer just a few miles from us and asked if I would be interested in processing some of their steel.

'What kind of tonnage?' I asked.

'Around 1,000 tonnes per month'.

My jaw hit the floor; it was like a message from heaven. That kind of tonnage would set us up more than just nicely.

Then reality kicked in. I suspected that our machinery would simply not be quick enough to justify the price he would demand for such large quantities of guaranteed work, and when he told me what price he was prepared to pay, it was so far below my threshold, there was no point in trying to negotiate. I had to decline. But we parted on really good terms. I suspect that if I had gone back to him, his door would have been open to me . . . and all because I was nice to a stranger who I thought was just trying to sell me something.

A SIMPLE QUESTION

A simple question to ask yourself is this: 'What did it cost me to be nice?' Or: 'What might it have cost me if I had been unpleasant?'

I still had faith that we would find a decent-sized contract, and it wasn't long before one came along in the form of processing the steel needed to make the early versions of satellite dishes that Sky was rolling out across the UK, millions of them.

Times were good.

Then the day came when the bubble burst. Unbeknownst to me, our client had been installing their own line. I cannot blame them for not telling me, because they couldn't afford to have me telling them to get lost until their own machine was up and running.

That contract had been worth a quarter of a million pounds a year to us, covering all of the overheads. One minute the work was there, the next it was gone.

Hindsight tells me I should have made some major cutbacks, let staff go, reduced my costs wherever I could. That would have been the sensible decision. But all of these people had families; how could I do that to them? I convinced myself that we could work our way through it. I would take on more sales staff; we would generate the turnover from somewhere else. That decision was not one of my finest; it was born more of hope than anticipation. I should have noticed that this time my 'faith' beacon was in the off position. The slippery slope had just tilted a little towards the abyss.

I took on a sales manager who was a really nice guy. But apart from creating a nice atmosphere in the office, he brought very little by way of new sales, barely making a dent in the volume we needed. My sales director wanted to let him go, but I wanted to give him a chance to succeed.

I guess that was because I have always believed that being nice is the most important trait of all. I believe that being that way would let me win through in the end. Perhaps it is true in the long run, over the course of a lifetime, but in the short term, I was mistaken. A healthy business is far better than one that has strangled itself on the altar of kindness and is no longer able to bring any good to anyone.

16

The Danger of Advertising (and Being Nice)

The only advertising that ever worked for us had been in the Yellow Pages. In my early years, my biggest customer had commissioned a press article about themselves. It was a PR exercise for them, paid for by the fact that their suppliers would take the opportunity to advertise alongside the editorial. The company wrote to me, telling me what they proposed and that they needed me to advertise to make the project a success.

The newspaper's advertising team had duly called me, and I had declined the opportunity. I'd had a few episodes in the past of these kind of things, and they had resulted in precisely zero. Besides, on this occasion this was my most valuable customer, and there was no way that I was going to advertise to my rivals who that customer was. I had told the newspaper that I did not want to go ahead, but now I had to explain myself to my client.

I decided to be honest and wrote to the company, explaining my reasons, and offering to donate what the advertising would have cost to a charity of their choosing. Two days later, my phone rang. It was their chairman. This was one of those *Oh shit, I have done it now* moments. He was surely about to tell me that I could kiss goodbye to all of their business.

'I've got your letter in front of me', he said. 'I must say that I'm surprised'.

'Surprised in what way?' I asked.

'Pleasantly surprised that someone would have the courtesy to write to me as opposed to simply ignoring our request'.

'Sorry, but I have a policy of not advertising in those things; I thought I should let you know that it's not about the money'.

'I understand. I don't really want to name a charity. Who you give the money to is up to you — do you like rugby?'

'Yes', I said, wondering where the conversation was leading.

'For my sins, I'm the chairman of M****** Rugby Club. If you're free on Saturday, I'd like to invite you to our next home game as my guest. Can you make it?'

That letter turned out to be one of the best pieces of selling I ever did. I went from being just another supplier to one favoured by the owner of the company. After that day, he stuck with me through thick and thin until he sold the business a few years later.

BUSINESS ISN'T BUSINESS IF YOU DON'T GET PAID

A few months after our biggest customer had walked away, we were still on a downward slide. Cash flow does not lie — if money is getting tighter, there is something wrong. It might mean the business is carrying too much stock or be a sign of something more serious.

I've already voiced my reservations about how factoring often leads to turnover chasing. This was happening to us. We took it on any order that came our way. There were few questions about the customers' ability to pay; we simply trusted that they would. Add that situation to the fact that we were advertising in the Yellow Pages, then we had the makings of a perfect storm.

When a company struggles to pay, its suppliers place a stop on their account. If they cannot find the money straight away, they have to find an alternative supplier.

In those days, where did they look to find that new supplier? Answer: The Yellow Pages.

Whose advertisement did they see front and centre? Answer: Mine!

Who was stupid enough to sell to them? Answer: Me!

That insight did not dawn on me until too late. A company which I had long since given up trying to sell to called me up out of the blue. Could we supply them?

Too right we could!

Two months later, they owed us £60,000. The invoice was due for payment that week. No payment came. They had gone into liquidation. In fairness, Judith, one half of the husband-and-wife team who owned the business, and the one who had placed the orders with me, was brave enough to face me. All I could do was give her a hug. How could I be angry? I'd lost £60,000; she had lost everything.

Only then did it occur to me that every single bad debt we'd suffered in the previous year had come from new clients, and all of them had come via the Yellow Pages. It was my fault for not bothering to check customers' ability to pay. I'd broken a fundamental rule: business is not business if you don't get paid.

17

Two Million in Two Days

**Just 'cos they have the law on their
side doesn't make them honest.**
—*Robin Hood (probably . . .)*

For several months, we did what we could to survive. There
isn't too much I'm proud of over that period, but we never gave
in to the temptation to be dishonest. We lost out on orders
because we were simply too expensive. Many of those orders
were going to rivals who I knew were putting their foot on the
scales when it came to advising their clients of the weight of
steel they had delivered. A low price multiplied by an inflated
quantity got them the value they needed to make a profit, and
usually a whole lot more. Even when times were bad, I could
never bring myself to do that.

We were going to be fighting an uphill battle if we were
to regain our previous success. By this time, I'd moved our
factoring agreement to a French bank. They had promised
a much more flexible facility and were by and large true to

their word. However, they were based in London. This was back in the days of snail mail. Money did not become available to us until the invoices we had raised were received by their office. More and more frequently I would have to drive to London in the early hours so that our invoices were in their post box when they opened up at 9:00 a.m. Those trips were usually as a result of having made someone a promise to pay them on that day or in the knowledge that a cheque we had issued was likely to bounce if I stayed at home. A tidal wave of disaster was gathering, but I was too pig-headed to acknowledge it, still determined not to give up.

Then one evening, a simple conversation changed my attitude. I was alone in my factory, just about to lock up and head for home, when a well-dressed man of about fifty walked through the door. I remembered him as a professional footballer. Now he headed up an engineering group.

'I thought I'd pop in to take a look at you. I'll come straight to the point: we would be keen to have a chat about buying your business. Have you thought about selling?'

'Not really', I said.

'Will you give it some thought and then maybe give me a call?' He gave me his card, and with that he was gone. I did give it some thought . . . all night.

By the next morning, I had made up my mind. I'd had enough of carrying the load. I wanted out. I called him that day, and the next, and the next and several times over the next month. Not once did I get through, and not once did he return my call. But he had sown the seed, and I realised it was time to move on.

I began to actively seek either someone to take an interest in the business or to take it over altogether. Being strangled for cash meant that all of our growth potential was on the back burner, so my sales pitch was that whoever took over the business would potentially make a good deal of money. I approached my biggest customer who had an appetite for acquisitions, and whilst their financial director thought it made sense, the chairman was somewhat put off by the fact that my factory was not as pristine as those in the rest of his group.

Eventually I struck it lucky. One of our suppliers was keen to get their hands on the kind of machinery we had, particularly because we had developed some unique processes which meant that we could reuse steel that otherwise would have been rejected. In short, we were pretty good at making a silk purse out of a sow's ear.

After a few months, we reached an agreement. They would purchase the company but not the factory. I would rent it to them on a 20-year lease. They didn't really like the rent, but it was better than them having to spend hundreds of thousands of pounds to move the machinery. I would continue working for them for two years, and if the company were successful, I would get a healthy bonus. There was no reason to think that it would not be successful given the purchasing power and resources that would be at my disposal.

As we finalised the details of our agreement, something happened to rain on my parade. A letter from the tax office dropped through the mailbox. They were demanding £90,000 in overdue tax. There was no way that I could not disclose this bombshell to my would-be purchaser.

'Sorry, Keith, but in that case, the deal is off'.

They didn't really give me a chance to finish my sentence, in which I would have told them not to worry because we were owed £120,000 in VAT, which would have been repayable in six weeks' time. (It's worth adding that I had already spoken to the tax office asking if they would offset one against the other, but they had refused).

Just two days later, the would-be buyer called me to say that maybe they had been a little too hasty, and that perhaps the deal could go ahead after all. But by then my teddybear was well and truly out of the pram; it was too late, and I told them so. Looking back, I could have salvaged the deal but chose to walk away. That was not one of my best decisions, and I reckon it cost me two million pounds. Losing two million in two days is not something I would recommend. But there are worse things that can happen.

SHERIFF OF NOTTINGHAM

Companies do not go bust for lack of cash, sales or profit. Those are symptoms, not reasons. Companies close down when the boss suddenly declares,

'I can't do this anymore'.

I'd heard the horror stories of companies going into liquidation. Frankly, there was no need for me to do that; there were enough assets to cover the money we owed. I called the bank and told them that we were going to close down. They were pretty horrified as they were owed £600,000.

'Don't worry', I said. 'The debtor book is worth a lot more than that, and I will get the money in for you, because if you try to do it yourself, the book of excuses will come out. I have a good relationship with most of the customers, and they are much more likely to pay if I'm the one doing the asking'.

'Do you want us to appoint administrators?' they asked.

I told them there was no need as there was plenty of money available to cover what they were owed and almost enough left over to pay the other creditors, and that was without selling off the stock. The bank accepted what I said, provided that I kept them informed as things went along.

Whilst I didn't appoint administrators, I *did* appoint an ex-insolvency practitioner as a consultant to help me with the closing down process. He wasn't cheap, and as he put it, insolvency practitioners hated what he did but could do nothing about it because he 'knew the law'. In essence, for a fee he was going to negotiate with the creditors and reschedule their payments in line with the money that came in after the bank had been paid.

One saving grace was that I have always believed in what I call 'rainy day management', and thus, I personally owned the factory and the machines within it.

As a landlord, I was owed a considerable sum in unpaid rent. Thus, in accordance with the law, I distrained upon the stock that sat in the factory. (Distraint is a robust piece of law which, for example, allows a hotel to seize your luggage if you don't pay their bill.)

I won't lie and say I was a popular lad amongst my creditors, because I certainly was not. The doors were blocked by lorry loads of rubble. The electricity was cut off, which meant I had to use a generator, and threats were coming in thick and fast. A well-known ex-heavyweight boxer was sent to my office to persuade me that his clients should be paid. He ended up paying several visits to me and went away empty-handed every time, because I could not do anything until the bank had been paid off.

'They've told me I have got to hit you, Keith, but I can't, because I like you'. We had become friends and stayed friends for years afterwards.

Gradually, with my customers' assistance, the amount I owed to the bank was reduced to just £5,000. Then, out of the blue, I received a phone call from my consultant.

'The bastards have appointed administrators', he said. 'They've waited until you collected all of their money but for the last few thousand, and just to be spiteful, they have chosen to do it while they still can because they are still owed a few measly quid'.

I called my bank manager.

'Why have you done that to me? I've collected your money for you'.

'Because we didn't like the way you did things'.

'It's funny how you didn't manage to do anything about it until you had your money, though, isn't it?' Perhaps I am being unfair, but to this day I wonder what was in it for them by way of commission.

The newly appointed administrators treated me as though I were something they had brought in on their shoe. Suffice to say that they were somewhat frustrated when they realised that I owned the factory and the machines and had distrained upon the stock. The only asset they could lay their hands on was around £250,000 of good debt still to come in plus a further £100,000 worth of debts that were being questioned by my more scurrilous customers.

They reported me to the department of trade, which interviewed me under caution for days. I found out later that they had trawled amongst my staff, trying to get them to speak against me, but no one did. No action was taken against me, but it still made my life very uncomfortable. And all of that because I didn't follow the usual way of closing the business, lining the pockets of certain establishments! More of that in a minute.

The far-from-delightful lady at the administrators consulted barristers, determined to find an error in my actions so that they could come after me personally. It took them several weeks to discover an obscure piece of English case law which suggested that a landlord's distraint on goods cannot be served on a Sunday. Guess which day I had chosen to exercise my distraint?

We finally settled the matter of the stock whereby they took possession of what remained, and I gave them a further cash settlement, which amounted to all of my savings. Despite the strained relationship between us, they accepted my offer to sell the stock on their behalf. They would have had no idea what they were selling, and I wanted to maximise the amount available for distribution to my creditors.

I may be coming across as somewhat bitter following this episode, and I certainly was at the time, but maybe not for the reason you might expect. When I closed there were sufficient assets to pay all of my creditors. I was owed £950,000. I owed £600,000 to the bank and about £250,000 to my creditors. After the stock had been sold and the administrators had received the VAT refund, they were sitting on at least £250,000 with which to pay the creditors.

I found out later that they passed the job of liquidating the company to one of the big four international accountancy firms. Why? There was nothing to liquidate. Everything had been sold off, and almost all of the money that could have been collected, had been.

So, what percentage of that £250,000 do you think was paid to the creditors?

The answer is . . . wait for a drum roll . . . a big, fat zero.

That's correct. Nothing was paid out.

Between them, they took it all in costs. They took all of the money, yet succeeded in laying the blame at my door.

'Why shouldn't they do that?' I hear you ask. 'You were the one who closed the business'.

Yes, I was, and I take my share of the blame in that regard, but on the day we closed, I owned three companies operating from that site, and there was a considerable amount of intercompany trading. When the accounts were offset against each other, the balance came to zero.

Let me explain . . . if your right hand owes your left hand £100, and your left hand owes your right hand £100, what is the debt? Zero. But the administrators would choose to present that as a £200 debt owed to the outside world. They elected not to show the contra element within my intercompany accounts. Instead, they added them together to make it look as though my company had debts of over £750,000 when £500,000 of it was simply my companies' debts to each other. They recorded a debt that did not exist.

I am no fan of insolvency practitioners. Yes, there are good ones, indeed some I count as friends, but too many are little more than licensed thieves. They took my creditors' money and laid the blame for doing so at my door. This is just a word of warning to those of you who might be tempted to consult with an insolvency practitioner. Too many will invite you into their office, smile as they put their arm around you and say: 'Don't worry, just sign here and kiss all your problems goodbye'. Poppycock! If ever there is anything to be aware of in the world of business, it is the smile on the face of the tiger.

REFLECTION

In my career, I have been fleeced and short-changed more times than I can remember, but few episodes left scars such as this.

What should I have done differently? How could I have avoided being painted as someone who had run away with a load of money when I hadn't?

The answer lies in the actions I took, or more accurately didn't take, more than a year previously. I should've cut my overheads to suit my income instead of trying to increase my income to exceed my overheads.

Overheads are much more difficult to reduce than they are to accumulate.

When the writing was on the wall . . . I should've read it!

Finally, a question.

When do you think that it's the best time to sell a business? When it's doing well and things are on the up, or when it's in decline and things are not so rosy? The answer should be pretty obvious, but how many of us try to cling on, hoping that an even higher peak will be reached only to find out too late that it has passed.

18

Be Nice (Part 2)

The next few weeks went by in a haze. I would be driving somewhere and then suddenly realise that I had nowhere to go and no one to see. For so long I'd been the CEO of a company, indeed a group of companies, and every day was always full-on. Now, all that had gone. I didn't know who I was anymore. I had lost my identity.

I spotted a job as a self-employed courier and applied. They invited me for an interview. The business owner was a larger-than-life character, and he liked me, and that was enough to get the job. I didn't have a van, so he pointed me in the direction of one of his clients who would rent one to me. In the weeks that followed, I would sit in the office until a job came in, then off I would go. Some days the jobs were local; on others I'd be sent much further afield.

On a couple of occasions, having been sitting doing nothing until three in the afternoon, I was sent to Aberdeen. Almost 900 miles in a van with no radio that barely did 60 miles an hour is a very long way, believe me, but at least I now had a purpose for driving somewhere.

Once I had paid the van rental and the cost of diesel, I found that I hadn't even earned minimum wage. Nevertheless, it got me out and about, and the long, silent hours at the wheel helped me get my head together.

I have to admit that sitting in that office for hours on end was, shall we say, entertaining. If ever Johnny Speight had modelled his Alf Garnett character on a real-life person, it was the boss of this courier firm. He told me that more than once he had gone home to tell his wife to pack their bags because he had lost their house in a game of cards. He meant it too. He was opinionated beyond belief and marginally more right-wing than Mussolini. When I told him that I was leaving, he shook my hand and said he would miss me because it was such a nice change to have some intelligent conversation around the office. As I recall, I barely ever got a word in edgeways! He was a lovable rogue, and I liked him. Life needs characters like that, however misguided we may think they are. I suppose 'rogue' was an appropriate term, as I read a few months later that he'd been had up for using his vans to smuggle duty-free goods in from Calais. Now I understood why the back office was so well stocked with cases of wine and spirits. There was I thinking he had a bit of a drink problem.

I learned a surprising lesson in those few weeks as a van driver . . . how rude people are to those whom they consider beneath them. When drivers came into my factory, I had always (I hope) been nice to them — after all, I needed them. I thought that such treatment was the norm. I soon found out that it wasn't. So many businesses I delivered to seemed to think I had just crawled out from under a rock, not worthy of demeaning themselves by speaking to or, heaven forbid, having a conversation with. The old adage: 'Be nice to people on the way up because you're sure to meet them on the way down', didn't seem to be working for me.

I needed to earn a living. I had machines that needed to be put somewhere, I still had customers who wanted to buy from me, and most importantly, I still had a few friends who would help me start again. The thing is, though, when you have gone from abundance down to a zero in a short space of time, stepping back into that world is as scary as hell. Gary, my long-time friend, once again came to my aid, and I started working from his factory.

Bless him for giving me the hand up that I so desperately needed. A few years previously, he had suffered a heart attack and had undergone triple bypass surgery. When he came back to work, he'd spoken of how his confidence had deserted him. He was afraid to commit money to deals which just a few months earlier would have been nothing out of the ordinary.

I had listened, but in truth, not understood. Boy, I did now! My confidence was shot. It helped that the courier company kept me on part-time while I was dipping my toe back into the water. Being like a rabbit caught in the headlights for half a week was more than enough to start.

FAMOUS FOR 15 MINUTES

For as long as I can remember, I've always been a singer. From maybe six or seven years old, they had me soloing in the choir of the Methodist chapel where I went to Sunday School. Apart from being in school plays, my first time onstage was as a 10-year-old at the local social club where they were holding their annual kids' Christmas party. Onstage were a compere and an organist — things weren't too sophisticated in 1965. The compere asked kids who wanted to sing to come forwards. I put my hand up and was eventually invited onstage. I sang "Yellow Submarine", a song to which I proudly knew all the words.

'Don't sit down, keep going', whispered the compere when the song had ended. 'Give them another one'. Then there was another and another and another.

As I got onstage, I vividly remember shaking with fear; I must have been sincerely regretting having raised my hand. I started to sing, and after just one line, it was as though someone had thrown a switch. I went from being scared to being absolutely elated. Fear had turned to excitement. I was in my element.

I have sung and entertained (I hope) ever since. After 55 years, the stage is one place where I'm in my comfort zone. And what about when things go wrong? That's part of the fun; otherwise it would be boring. I love the thrill, knowing that if something goes wrong, I'll be able to deal with it, usually with laughter. And that brings me back to my 'Famous for 15 minutes story'.

After my business closed, one of the things I could still do to earn money was to sing. So, I did. I toured pubs and clubs as a soloist. It wasn't long before I grew to hate doing it, but the audience never knew, and I always seemed to be invited back.

I remember playing one particular club, where the entrance onto the stage was, unusually, not from the side but through a door directly behind the centre of the stage. The master of ceremonies gave me a big introduction, and I, not being used to such effusive generosity, bounded on stage full of enthusiasm. Trouble was, I hadn't noticed just how low the doorway was. I banged my head, and it knocked me flat on the floor.

It didn't knock me out; it just bloody hurt. I didn't have a lot of choice but to make a joke of it, and everyone laughed.

I forgot about that door and did the same thing again the following year. By then, everyone thought it was part of my act, but it wasn't. Quite by mistake I was becoming an entertainer as opposed to a singer, and that's what I've been ever since.

To promote my show-biz career, I used to enter talent shows. These were national affairs that would attract talent from all over the country. They were a bit like a cheap version of *The X Factor*, I guess. I never won one, but I regularly reached the finals, which were usually covered by the press. I saw it as good exposure for getting higher-paid work.

I remember on one occasion *The Stage and Television Today* newspaper described my voice as 'mellifluous' . . . I had to look it up.

There was a sizeable contest to be held in Southport. The day came for the first round, and I left work early to get there in plenty of time. It was late afternoon, and I was trying to find the venue without success, so I thought I would give them a call to find out exactly where they were.

'Is that the Floral Hall?'

'Yes, how can I help?'

'I'm performing in the talent show tonight and can't seem to find you'.

'We're right on the seafront'.

'I can't see you'.

'We're by the lake'.

'What lake? I can't see a lake'.

'It's by the pier'.

Now, piers are pretty hard to miss in a seaside town. I couldn't see one, and it began to dawn on me that the young lady I was listening to seemed to be a long way from home. Her North-West accent seemed way out of place for someone in Southend. And then it hit me . . . *She* wasn't a long way from home at all, I was in the wrong place. She was in Southport; I was in Southend, the wrong end of the country!

I had to admit my mistake and asked her to ask the theatre manager to scrub my name from the list. I turned around and headed for home, feeling something of a plonker. Correction! A complete plonker! Still, no harm done; no one need know. After 20 minutes, I was making my way back towards London when a thought struck me. I called the theatre again and was put through to the manager.

'I'm the idiot who was supposed to be performing tonight but who's gone to the wrong end of the country, and I know I've asked you to take my name off the list, but can I still go on if I can get there in time?'

'I guess so', he said, doubtfully but kindly. That was it, foot to the floor and hope that the M25 would be kind during rush hour.

I don't know what time I got there; I just know it was late. They were hoping that I would arrive, as the MC had told the whole theatre audience of my exploits. I ran in to the front entrance and told the door staff who I was, but I suspect they had already guessed.

'He's here!' said a voice over the P.A. system. It was the compere. 'Come on mate, you're on'.

The crowd roared as I ran through the auditorium and jumped onto the stage, breathless. I know I did two songs, but I only remember one of them. It was Smokey Robinson's "The Tracks of My Tears".

I went down a storm. Maybe it was because I was good, or more likely, it was just a sympathy vote for the idiot who had just driven from the other end of the country. Who knew? Who cared? Years later, I used to say to some of the youngsters who were on my record label (that is another story) that **nothing you squirt up your nose or jab in your arm will ever repeat what an audience can do for you**. The magic of that whole theatre roaring in approval ranks up there as one of the high points of my stage career.

It was not just the audience who knew of my extended journey; the local press were there too. They reported it, and the next day the nationals picked it up. If I remember rightly, there were pieces in quite a few of the tabloids, and I shared a full page in the *Daily Star* with Lady Di. One of us appeared as a fool — I will leave you to guess which — but my headline read 'The Treks of My Tears'.

They say that any form of publicity is good publicity. I braced myself in anticipation of the phone ringing off the hook, as my path to stardom would begin. I am still waiting.

REFLECTION

I said earlier that nothing really bothers me if things go wrong on stage. Well, after you have made yourself look such a chump in front of the whole world, why would it? We can only fall so far, and we have only failed if we don't get up, even knowing that chances are we will fall again, and again, and again.

That's the whole point. Life isn't about everything being tickety-boo 24/7 for all of your life. It's about the lessons that you learn. It's all part of growing. All our lives, like it or not, we are at some stage of growing, and if we aren't growing, we are dying. Just think of the line in *The Shawshank Redemption*: 'Get busy living or get busy dying'.

I have spoken about the essential traits of *balls* and *imagination* that an entrepreneur needs. Well, I want to add to the list . . . keep a sense of humour; don't be afraid to laugh at yourself. Be like a clown; if you fall, get up, dust yourself down and start over. I did, time and time again. And I know for sure that smilers win!

19

Give Up or Get Up

The months rolled by, and gradually my confidence started to come back. My overheads were next to nothing; I had two or three great customers. I was making money, *good* money, by working just a couple of hours a day. I'd say that was the best of it, and yet it was perhaps the worst of it. My mum used to say: 'The devil makes work for idle hands'. And I guess that happened to me. I didn't turn to crime, but I did lose my moral compass. In short, I ran away with a younger woman and bought a motorbike. I hurt a lot of people during that period in my life. It's a time that I'm not proud of. Everything that happened was all on me, and I still carry the guilt.

It took a year or so, but gradually when my confidence did come back, it wasn't the balls-out gung-ho confidence I'd had in my twenties but a kind of quiet confidence that things would be OK. My honeymoon period of making good money with just a few hours' work was also long gone. I was having to work for every penny I earned. Suppliers were starting to extend me credit again, but the great deals I used to be able to do had become a thing of the past. Margins were getting ever tighter, and customers were demanding instant service.

As good as my friends were to me, I couldn't ask any more of them. It was time to open my own production facility again. I only needed four or five thousand square feet and found an ideal place just a stone's throw from where I had been working.

I spent a week installing one of the only machines I still had. It was Friday afternoon, and I was just making the finishing touches, so as to be able to start production on the following Monday, when an old friend walked in.

'Hello Keith, long time no see', he said. 'I heard you'd just opened up again, so I thought I'd pop in to see how you are going'. It was nice to see him, but I thought it a little strange, since I hadn't seen him in years. He and his friend seemed really interested in the machinery I had just installed. After they had strolled around with me for a while, they suddenly left as abruptly as they had arrived.

On the following Monday I came to work, planning to run the machine on my own for a few weeks until I could find an operator for it. But as soon as I opened the door, I realised that finding an operator was the least of my problems. All, and I mean ALL, of the tooling to my machine had been stolen. Without it, the machine might as well have been a pile of scrap.

I am not saying that it was this guy, but I was well aware that one of his close relatives would've had need of identical tooling to mine, and my instincts were now screaming at me that he had been casing the joint when he visited me. I couldn't prove it, and frankly was in no state to go round there with a baseball bat. Besides, with nothing to go on but a feeling, what could I have done?

I wasn't insured, and to replace what had been stolen with new tooling would take many weeks and tens of thousands of pounds.

Shit! I could either give up or get up.

In a way, that's what this whole book is about: those circumstances that happen when we least expect them. An illness, a marriage breakup, the loss of someone close to us or a bankruptcy can stop us dead in our tracks. In this case, it was theft.

I have no doubt that the theft was targeted. The bastards who broke into my factory took precisely the tooling used by one specific type of machine. The replacement value of what they had stolen easily ran into five figures, several times over. I would not only have to find money I hadn't got to replace it, but they had taken away my means of making that money in the first place. As I said, it was one of those times to make a choice. **Give up or get up.**

The decision wasn't that hard.

I had no other strings to my bow, and therefore no choice but to find my way out of it.

No matter where I looked, there was no tooling to be had on the second-hand market. However, the thieves had kindly left behind a single set of tools which didn't fit my machine. I managed to find a company that could re-engineer them for me so that they'd fit. They charged me an arm and a leg, but at least they got the job done quickly instead of my having to wait three months for a new set to be made. After two weeks of very expensive frustration, I was finally back in production.

Looking back, it was nothing compared to some of the other traumas that I went through over the years, and yet in a way, it was just as threatening. I'd had my means of income removed overnight.

How many times have we heard the expression *'It's an ill wind that blows no one any good'*. On this occasion, being knocked on my backside and then getting up turned out well. The stolen tooling had been designed to do certain jobs. The replacement tooling I had was far flimsier and designed for much smaller tasks. Then fate dealt me a kindly hand when I was asked to take in a long-term contract. My stolen tooling could not have done the job, and I would have had to decline the order, but this flimsy tooling was absolutely made for it. Over the next few years, we produced a huge amount for this client. We were good at it, and it became one of our principal products. Though they certainly hadn't meant to, the thieving so-and-sos had done me a favour. As I said, *it's an ill wind that blows no one any good*.

It's strange how when we make that decision to say 'Damn it! Let's carry on', we get rewarded. Whoever it was who said that 'The strongest oak trees grow in the weakest soil' was right.

We came out of the situation stronger than we could have ever imagined. It was back to having faith again. Before the book and film *The Secret* emerged, I had barely heard of the *law of attraction*; I used to call it the 'law of expectation'; indeed, I still call it that.

NOW FOR THE WOO-WOO

Shortly after setting up my first business, I saw an ad offering a book called *The Lazy Man's Way to Riches*. That was the first time I had ever come across the law of attraction, or expectation. The advertisement said that people are too busy working to make any money. That rang true for me, so I bought the book. I was probably sceptical as to the ideas it expressed, but I had nothing to lose, so I decided to do as it suggested.

The book instructed me to write something called affirmations. I'd never heard of such things. But nevertheless, I wrote some down in a small black book which I was to carry with me everywhere I went. The affirmations were to be written in the present tense, as though what I wanted was already in existence. I was to read them at least once a day.

Part of me thought it was a load of hogwash. The other part of me thought that there might be something in it, and I was ambitious. I reached a compromise between my ambition and scepticism by keeping my black book a secret. I told no one, not even my closest family.

I kept that book with me for over a year until gradually it fell into disuse, ending up forgotten at the back of a drawer somewhere. Decades later, I found it. I knew instantly what it was; I read through it, smiling at the goals I'd had as a much younger man. And then it hit me. I had achieved every single one of those goals except one — wanting a farm. I didn't get the farm, but I do live in a farming village where every newcomer thinks that ours is the farmhouse. That's close enough, in my book . . . all of the benefits and none of the headaches.

20

Time Passes

I can't say that our growth over the next four years was spectacular, especially when compared to my previous attempt. We were making money, and I'd accumulated some apparently valuable assets. Would anyone have wanted to buy them? Probably not. What I'd built was not so much a business, as more of a well-paid job.

Businesses start on a dream and end on a nightmare. When we start out, we are full of dreams and ambition, underpinned by a healthy dose of optimism. And let's face it, that last ingredient is super-important, because without it, dreams and ambitions will stay *dreams and ambitions*. Optimism tells us we can win. We walk to the edge of the diving board and leap into the unknown, sure that our abilities and good fortune will carry us aloft.

If we survive that first terrifying leap, we gradually start to make money and accumulate assets. Starting out, we have little to lose, but after a while, protecting what we have starts to become more important. It's not nearly so exciting to go to work every day to protect what we have, as opposed to making more. We build a business so that we can control our destiny, be free of tyrannical bosses and do what we want to do when we want to do it.

And thereby hangs the illusion. We started building a dream, only to find in so many cases that instead of building a dream, we have built a nightmare. We have built our own version of Frankenstein's monster. We don't control it — it controls us. We are a prisoner held hostage to its needs. Everything we do revolves around the business. This happened to me more than once, despite the fact that I promised myself that it wouldn't, but it always did. It was my source of income, my identity, my pain and anguish and, eventually, my source of despair.

With hindsight (that greatest or maybe most useless of management tools), I could have been a far better delegator than I was. I simply didn't trust those around me sufficiently to let them get on with it. It was quicker to do a job myself than to let someone else take slightly longer to do it. That's a recipe for disaster in itself, but I simply couldn't let go. Eight-hour days turned into ten-, then twelve- and then eventually eighteen-hour days. Burnout beckoned.

Delegation wasn't my only problem. Too often, I accepted second-best from my staff, justifying my reaction to poor performance by telling myself that they were doing their best, so that was OK. But here's the thing: it was not OK. It was eventually going to lead to the company's collapse.

There is one more thing that underpinned all of this striving, angst and long hours. I believed then, and for many years afterwards, that my hapiness depended on how much money I had. I would have lost a great deal more than this business before I realised how wrong I was. My happiness did not lie at the end of a financial rainbow; it lay within me.

It was my decision to make: whether to be happy or not. I know that many will find that hard to accept. I can only say that it turned out true for ME, and I believe it can be equally true for anyone. External factors are exactly that — external.

WATERSHED MOMENTS

There comes a point when fortunes change, be that for the better or worse. An event or even a conversation might be something profound, or something much more subtle, and only with the benefit of hindsight can we identify it as a watershed moment.

I was helping out on a steel rolling mill to meet an urgent order. Howard, the machine operator, suddenly turned to me, his face distorted in dismay. He held his hand out — his thumb was completely sheared off, left hanging by the skin of one side.

My instinct was to put it back into place, and that is precisely what I did, holding it there until an ambulance arrived. Howard spent several weeks in hospital after surgery had reattached his thumb. Leeches were applied to his arm so as to keep his blood thin enough to allow the procedure to succeed. Yuk! They must have worked, because by the time he left hospital, Howard was still in possession of a slightly altered, but nevertheless functional, thumb. I continued to pay his wages.

Now, the only person who could operate the rolling mill for the foreseeable future was yours truly. I knew I was poor at delegating, but even I knew that would not be sustainable.

Operating a machine of this type is half skill and half art. It wasn't easy to find a replacement for Howard, but eventually I found Tony, who had the necessary experience. Although he did things differently (because you can't teach an old dog new tricks), he was good at the job. The problem was, the company was paying him and still paying Howard. That couldn't go on forever, but as I saw it, there was no other option.

Looking back, we should have helped Howard over the financial blow while he waited for his insurance claim to come through. As it was, all we did was reduce the value of his claim from the insurance company, effectively saving them a substantial amount of money, which he could have claimed as lost wages. Would they compensate the company for having done that? Er, no!

Howard returned to work about a year later. What was I to do, tell him there was no job? Sack the guy who had admirably filled in for him? No. Instead I employed both of them, staggering their hours by an hour at each end of the day so that, in effect, I had ten hours of production with them working together for eight of those hours. It was a disaster; production actually went down. On the face of it, they tried to pull together, and to my knowledge at least, they never fell out. But to the company, it was a car crash.

REFLECTION

What should I have done? I should have continuously made it clear to the new guy, not just at the beginning, but month by month, that this was a temporary contract. If he had been clearly better than the guy he replaced, I should have created two jobs where there was previously one and then made one of those jobs redundant. What I did was take the 'nice guy' coward's way out and employed them both, ultimately the kind of poor management that led to them both losing their job, along with all of their colleagues.

THE DEMON DRINK: EPISODE 1

My lead operator, and in my absence, de facto works manager, had moved some 50 miles away. I thought it was too far to commute, but he assured me that it would be OK, and in fairness, the previous couple of years had proven him correct. He wasn't just good at what he did, he was *very* good at what he did.

There were quicker operators than he, a lot quicker. But what the company got from him was absolutely top-notch quality. Not once did we ever suffer a rejected product that had been a result of his poor workmanship. And if ever a rejection did happen, he was always the first to want to know why it had occurred. He was proud of the work that he produced. Quality gurus can come up with all the jobsworth quality-control bullshit they like, but they will never beat the quality achieved by a craftsman who is proud of what he produces. In short, this man was one of the mainstays of the business as far as the factory was concerned and was paid accordingly.

However, unbeknownst to me, he'd developed a drink problem and had fallen into the habit of stopping on the way home from work to sit in his car at the side of the road, consuming several cans of beer. Of course, one day he was spotted. He came to me the following day and handed in his notice. He was honest and told me the reason.

'There is simply no way I can get here once I've lost my licence', he said.

'We will find a way'. I was determined not to lose him.

We did find a way. Before he was due in court, he found a neighbour who needed a job, and who would drive him to and from work. The neighbour had no skills that the company could use, so I took him on as a general labourer even though he had medical issues that would preclude him from doing parts of the job. In reality, I paid for a chauffeur until my operator got his licence back, and in truth I think he was glad to go after that.

His presence had caused resentment amongst others on the team, not simply because he didn't have the skills to pull his weight (they were unaware of his medical problems) but also because I was seen to favour someone to such an extent that I provided them with a chauffeur. Who could blame them?

THE DEMON DRINK: EPISODE 2

Alcohol was to cause another problem. I was approached by the general manager of one of my competitors. He was, he said, extremely unhappy at work. He felt that his efforts alone were earning all of the money the company made, while his directors sat back and did nothing except demand that he made them more. If what he said was true, what a sad state of affairs that the directors of a company would allow an environment to exist whereby such feelings could take root and grow.

Given my experience of sales managers, it took him a while to persuade me that he could bring substantial orders if I gave him a chance. Eventually I gave in, and to my surprise, his employers didn't fight to keep him. He was soon ensconced in our office, brimming with enthusiasm and gratitude. It cost the company a car and a sizeable salary, but what the heck, we needed the extra turnover that he promised.

He was a nice lad, but so sad and troubled in many ways. At first, he was gushing with compliments about the quality of our workmanship and saying that as soon as his clients saw it, they would be eager to become customers.

The problem was, for all of his good intentions, I can't remember a single new client being won, and what was worse, my own customers didn't take to him. That wasn't his fault — I should've considered how they might react before I gave him the green light.

I guess that one of my strongest traits is also a major weakness. I am tolerant with everyone except myself. I could forgive him for the way he was and choose to see his good side. But my clients could not or would not.

And then there was the demon drink. I'd had my suspicions, and then I witnessed him turning up for work, sneaking into the empty reception, and hiding an open can of super-strength lager behind one of the sofas, clearly intending to have a sneaky swig when he passed by. He would have gotten quite a shock when he found my business card neatly placed on top of the half-empty can. He never said anything, nor did I.

Perhaps I should have, either to admonish him or better understand why he felt the need. He never repeated the exercise, but not long afterwards, he passed out at the wheel of his car and half-demolished a small church. The traffic police visited the office, as that was where the car was registered. I quietly asked them if he had been drinking and was surprised when told that drink had not been a factor.

Another month went by. Then he stopped coming to work, citing illness. I paid him for a while, but after a few months when he still hadn't returned, we had to agree that it was game over. He had been living on his nerves, and he admitted he was in no state to hold down a job.

A few months later, I heard the sad news that he had taken his own life. At his funeral, his distraught mother came to me and thanked me, telling me that I was the only one who had been kind to him for so many years. I didn't think I had been particularly kind to him. Whatever his faults, no one should feel so low that they take their own life. If I could turn back the clock, I would have done more for him, but would that simply have delayed the inevitable? I'll never know, but I cannot help thinking that I should have tried. Bless him, wherever he is.

AND THEN THERE WAS THE GAMBLER

He was a real charmer, and by all accounts good at his job. He'd worked for a few of our competitors as a salesman, and I liked him. On one occasion he'd asked me to lend him some money as, somewhat bizarrely, he had an opportunity to buy a job lot of garden tools. It wasn't a huge amount, so I said yes.

It took him a few weeks longer than he'd promised to pay me back, but pay me back he did. Not long after that, he came to work for us as sales manager. He and I got on really well, regularly socialising, and in that time I got to know quite a few of his friends. Instead of a bog-standard company car, he wanted a sporty car because it helped him with the ladies — such was his life.

At first, he did well; his sales were growing, and several new accounts were being opened. There was, however, one thing that I noticed. My journey home from the office normally took me past a casino. And night after night, parked right outside, front and centre, was his car. More concerning were a couple of occasions when I saw it outside during working hours. When I asked him about it, he told me that he liked to go there to chill out on his way home.

The nature of every relationship between two people on the same team is that there has to be trust. Alarm bells were ringing, but I was choosing to ignore them, determined as usual to see only the good in people. In the two months he had been with us, he had produced some impressive sales figures, after all.

He had brought a new client based in Norfolk and announced that he intended to drive the eight-hour round trip to pay them a visit. I saw no reason to disapprove. But after his trip, he didn't show up for work the next day, or the next or the next. All of our calls to him remained unanswered.

I called the client, who told me that he had never had an appointment with her. He had called her, but instead of making an appointment, he had asked her to say that he had been there if I should happen to call. Now that he'd disappeared, and she understood that I was worried, she'd no reason to lie. Indeed, if I had asked on the day he was supposed to have been there, she had made up her mind that she wouldn't lie anyway.

Weeks went by, and he had simply disappeared. So, too, had his company car. The great sales he had achieved started to fall due for payment. One of those sales was worth a substantial amount of money. In the steel industry it is common practice to have to chase for the money that you are owed. Companies that pay their bills without being asked are as rare as hens' teeth and highly prized. This client was not one of those; we had to call them, only to be told, 'According to our records, there is nothing outstanding'.

The truth rapidly emerged. They had indeed placed an order for the item shown on our invoice but had rejected the entire consignment. Apparently, we had collected it. No replacement was needed, as they had been singularly unimpressed by our quality and placed their order elsewhere.

We finally traced the haulier that had collected the goods, and they informed us that they had taken them to their storage warehouse, where they were being held on the say-so of our sales manager. They asked if we would mind paying their invoice. After a painful amount of money had changed hands, we had the consignment delivered back to our works.

As soon as it arrived, the team in the factory recognised it. They had wondered why it had ever been dispatched in the first place, as it was nothing like the specification that had been ordered. But because the sales manager 'knew the job and the customer so well' and had assured them that it would be acceptable, they went ahead and processed the whole consignment, turning perfectly good steel into what was effectively scrap.

We tried to salvage what we could, but re-processing it would have cost more than it was worth. It was one we had to take on the chin.

Still there was no sign of my errant sales manager and, more importantly, his car. I contacted the garage who had sold it to us and asked them to repossess it, assuring them that we would pay any losses incurred in reselling it. I never saw that sales manager again, but a couple of years later, I did in fact hear from him in a roundabout way.

It turned out that when I had lent him money, I had been the exception to the rule in that amongst all of his friends and relatives, I had been the only one he had ever paid back. He had borrowed money from all of them to feed his gambling habit, and I suspect the garden tools story he'd told me was one of several ploys he had used. In the end, it all added up to fraud, and he was sent to prison.

After coming out of prison and applying for a job, he had somewhat audaciously given my name as a reference. The best bit was that the job was in a bank call centre. Even after all that had happened, he had done his time, so I didn't want to bad-mouth him. I did in fact provide a reference; it was, however, very carefully worded!

I guess, with a few exceptions, I'd never been good at employing sales people. All in all, I reckon my inability to find the right people probably put me back at least a million pounds behind where I would have been if I had never employed them.

21

Not All Rules Are for Breaking

I have never been one of those people who follow the law to the letter. Too much of it is jobsworth to my way of thinking. That is not to say that I go out to break the law; I just don't particularly follow bullshit rules.

After a good deal of pressure over a couple of years, our landlord finally agreed to re-roof the factory that by now Gary and I shared. The appointed contractor had appointed a subcontractor, who had appointed another subcontractor to actually carry out the work. If ever there was a recipe for cutting corners, this was it.

The factory consisted of two separate bays; it was going to take a week for each of them. They started on Gary's bay first. After a couple of days, it was apparent that speed was king, with quality not even a close second. When stripping off the old roofing sheets, they simply tipped the debris down onto the factory floor, or machinery, or whoever happened to be standing below.

That was bad enough, but on the third day, I looked up to see that in the interest of speed, they had dispensed with using safety netting. There was someone I didn't recognise standing in the middle of my part of the factory, looking up at them as they worked. I assumed he was their boss and marched up to him. It's not very often that I'm quite as forthright as I was on this occasion.

'If you think when they come over to my side of the factory, they're going to do what they're doing without putting up safety netting, you can think again', I said.

'I'm glad you said that', he replied. 'I'm the factory inspector'.

He stopped them working until they'd put up the required safety netting. Trying to save time cost them several days, as they had to wait for his return to inspect the netting before they were allowed to continue.

The following week, I was watching, dismayed that they continued to pour their debris into what was now our side of the factory when a young lad of about 18 or 19 came crashing through the roof. It happened in an instant; with no chance of saving himself, he fell backwards into the safety netting, above where a large piece of machinery awaited his arrival some 30 feet below. The lad had been lucky. At the very least, chances are he would probably have been in a wheelchair for the rest of his life.

Once completed, the new roof was a revelation. Now we didn't have to leave gaps in our stock at points where water came in, and we could carry even more. The trouble is stock costs money when it is just sitting there. There is an accounting ratio called stock turn, which is the sales achieved in a given period, divided by the stock level that is carried. Our stock turn was usually pretty good at around twenty-four times a year.

The newfound extra space meant more stock, which in itself would have been fine if we had been achieving more sales. But we weren't. What the heck, we were making money. Who cared?

NONE SO BLIND AS THOSE WHO DO NOT WANT TO SEE

There was a tidal wave building up somewhere on the horizon, and it was heading my way. Even though I had accounting and management qualifications, I had always run my businesses on instinct, which had rarely let me down. But now I wasn't heeding it.

I'd never heard of things like SWOT (strengths, weaknesses, opportunities and threats) analysis. Perhaps if I had used such tools, things might have been different. We had been factoring or invoice discounting our sales for quite a long time; it was an expensive but necessary evil. What it took from the gross margin didn't look so bad, but the net margin shrank to little above zero.

A HOARDER OF OVERHEADS

Everyone has days when they question just how well, or perhaps not so well, they are doing. I remember more than once going through the company's overheads determined to make cuts. Examining the figures line by line, everything I saw I considered uncuttable. I had become a hoarder of overheads. They were mine, and I didn't want to part with them. Anyway, the largest overhead was yours truly, and I couldn't very well sack myself.

Those are the times when any boss with a heart looks at their staff and wonders how devastating it would be to their families if any one of them should lose their job. I have been told more than once that one of my best traits is my capacity for empathy. But empathy is a double-edged sword. What I like to call my empathy bone has more than once led to catastrophe.

For a year or more, we had been losing an average of one contract every month, as our customers switched their production to China. Four out of my five top customers had disappeared. Either we needed to generate more sales or I needed to downsize my workforce. Ever bullish, I took on yet another sales manager. He had a track record of being able to sell, but I was warned that he could be a loose cannon, sometimes working on really low margins or buying material that just went into stock as opposed to being resold.

Nevertheless, he joined us, and things looked bright. The turnover was climbing, and the consequent need for extra cash was being met by the fact that we were factoring our invoices. Optimism had once again walked through the doors. But, and it's a huge 'but', there is an insidious problem with factoring or invoice discounting that can do untold damage. I have written about this elsewhere, but it bears repeating.

Factoring or invoice discounting is fine when the turnover is growing, and the borrowings are well within the ceiling set by the lender. But when that ceiling is reached and the turnover dips, the eyes of the management are taken from the bottom line and fixed firmly on the turnover . . . turnover at any price.

I had been down this road and should have known better. Bad debts started to come in with alarming regularity, and we began to flounder. Often, I would arrive at the office, and my secretary would take a deep breath before telling me that the bank had removed a five-figure sum from our borrowing facility overnight because they had heard a rumour about one of our customers.

Because cash flow was already tight, I had promised to pay that money to my suppliers on that very day in anticipation of it being available. I would then spend the next several hours trying to convince the bank of their mistake, and usually I succeeded. But by then it was maybe three or four in the afternoon. How successful can any business hope to be when the managing director is forced to spend six or seven hours a day, sometimes several days a week, firefighting in this way?

We were achieving more turnover, but the margins were such that it was barely profitable, if at all. Longstanding clients were demanding price reductions, as they had been offered cheaper alternatives. Yet this was at a time when our buying prices were on the rise.

A significant factor in us having to pay higher prices was that the pool of companies willing to sell to us was growing steadily smaller. Our falling credit rating was taking its toll. First to jump ship were those who allowed us the best margins; now we were having to pay a premium to buy the same goods through a third party. We had failed to maintain our credit rating. Things were becoming unsustainable.

BUST TO BREAKDOWN

My stress levels were through the roof. I was doing my best to keep everyone in a job, using my credit cards to meet the wages bill. They say that businesses go bust for lack of profit or lack of cash. I do not agree — to me, as I said earlier, those things are symptoms. Businesses go bust when the boss gets up one morning and says, 'I can't do this anymore'. And that is what happened to me.

The day came when an insolvency practitioner was the only answer. It was Monday, and I was to meet him at 6:30 a.m. in my office, before everyone arrived. I got there early and waited. Suddenly, I began to shake uncontrollably. My body no longer belonged to me — it had shut down. My brain simply could no longer process what was going on. I was having a breakdown.

I took the coward's way out and met him away from the office, leaving him to go back to break the news to my staff. I was mentally and physically broken. I was 'visited' by certain creditors, but I had nothing to give; all I had was gone. Some of them offered to help me, and to their absolute discredit, they lined their own pockets while I was in no state to stop them. I was ashamed beyond words.

I had taken money from my friends. Someone told me not to worry because what happened was simply tomorrow's chip paper. (Younger readers may not be aware that fish and chip takeaways used to be wrapped in the previous day's newspapers). Looking back, he had a point, but it was no consolation. The company went into liquidation, and I was required to attend the creditors' meeting. On the morning it was set to take place, my wife said,

'You're dreading it, aren't you?'

'Yes', I replied, 'but not half as much as I've been dreading going to work on Monday mornings for the last six months'.

Some forgave me, others hated me, some probably fiddled their insurance to make sure they got paid. But no one beat me up; I did a great job of that on myself. Yet within all of that stress, shame and anxiety lay lessons . . . I just needed to find them.

22

Integrity, the Priceless Asset

I was at the bottom of nowhere to go. That sounds like some kind of a contrived line, but it was simply the way I felt. I needed a job, but it was back to the same old not-so-merry-go-round.

Who wants to employ a failure? And boy, was I wearing that label front and centre. I was offered work in my old trade but couldn't face going back. There was no choice but to go for commission-only jobs, but even they were hard to come by. After several weeks of trying, I was offered a job selling business telephone lines. I remember sitting in my car having been offered the job and sobbing like a baby in absolute relief.

The training lasted a few days. Whilst training, I'd witnessed a call centre in action for the first time. Theirs was a high-pressure numbers game, in which the youngsters (they were all youngsters) were expected to make cold call after cold call, no let up, no breaks, no letting prospects off the hook until they had fixed an appointment for a field sales representative like me to visit a prospect and close the sale. I was uneasy with the way they worked, but what choice did I have? I had to give it a go.

I didn't last very long. I'd visit prospects who insisted they had not made an appointment or who were simply not there. Then I was detailed to visit a Chinese restaurant. The owner was really nice and gave me tea as we chatted.

I explained what signing up with us could do for his business, but he politely told me that it wasn't for him. My uneasiness kicked into overdrive: my instructions were such that if a prospect said no, then while I was still with them, I had to call the sales manager (the one with the whip in the call centre) and tell him so that he could try to persuade the client to change his mind. I had managed to duck out of doing so over the previous couple of weeks, but this time there was no avoiding it. So, I made the call.

'Mr So-and-so has listened to what we have to offer, but he has decided it's not for him'.

'Put him on'.

I could hear most of what was said by the sales manager, who truly believed he was God's gift to selling. After having tried his best high-pressure selling techniques, in response to the client politely repeating that he did not wish to go ahead, this arrogant prick grew steadily more and more belligerent, accusing this nice man of wasting his and his team's time.

When the conversation ended, the only thing that Mr Arrogant Prick had achieved was alienating a prospect who might have become a client in the future.

The 'no longer ever going to be a client' was perplexed. 'Keith, you are a nice man', he said, sadly. 'Why are you working for someone like that?'

'I'm not', I replied. 'Having heard the way he spoke to you, I want no part of that kind of thing. I'm resigning'. We parted on good terms.

Upon hearing the news that I was resigning, effective immediately, Mr Arrogant Prick tried to use his best techniques to persuade me to stay. He was going on and on until, I have to admit, I used a very unoriginal line: 'What part of *I resign* don't you understand?'

I was out of work, again! But this time, I didn't have to wait long to get my next chance; I'd discovered that I could sell. But here's the thing: I'm not one of those fine-mouthed people who can sell anything to anybody; I can only sell what I believe will be of benefit to my prospect. That theme has run through all of my selling over the last twenty years. It might be argued that it has cost me dearly, but at least I can look in the mirror.

Let me give you a couple of examples.

My second post demise job saw me working for The Credit Protection Association, selling credit management services to UK businesses. When I started, I had holes in the soles of my shoes and had to remember to keep my feet flat on the floor so as not to show how successful I was when presenting my wares. The job was commission only, but this time I was selling something I believed in, I'd seen first hand just how good it was and it turned out that I was pretty good at it. For a couple of years, I was genuinely helping my clients. One of my 'closes' was 'It's good, isn't it? But you need to know this, it's a fabulous service, and there's nothing like it on the market, but if you don't use it . . . you'll waste your money'. The response was usually 'I will use it, I will. Where do I sign?'

Gradually I began to realise that despite my warnings, too many of those who signed up were either not using the system properly or not using it at all. As soon as I got an inkling that this would be the case, I found that I couldn't close the deal. My performance began to falter, until in the end I was earning nothing. I was living on thin air. It was time to move on. David Baber, the chairman of the company was understanding and incredibly supportive and kind to me at that time. I am forever in his debt.

I had been told that I'd be a shoo-in to sell advertising. Big mistake. Having done a few weeks' training, I was let loose selling advertising to small businesses. I guess I was OK at it, but my heart wasn't in it. Like my last 'job', appointment-making was a nightmare, and unlike my last job, when I made a sale, the commission was tiny. But I soldiered on. Beggars can't be choosers, right?

And then I met Steve. He ran a small double-glazing company and had recently downsized. We sat in his kitchen and got on famously from the start. He told me why he had downsized and how business was going, and I told him of my history and why I'd ended up selling advertising. After two rounds of coffee, he invited me to deliver my pitch. Then, having listened to every word, he floored me.

'OK, Keith', he said, 'we've shared our stories, and I know that you were in business for all those years. I'll go by your recommendation. If I were offering this to you, would you go for it?'

I had a choice. Lie to get the order, or I could tell the truth.

'No', I said, 'I wouldn't'.

Outside on his driveway, I called the office and resigned.

The owner of the company called me later that day.

'Of all the people I have taken on over the last year, you are the one who has the bang-on character to make a go of this. Why the heck are you leaving?'

Although I declined to go back, it was nice to hear. With no job and no money, my confidence needed all the help it could get.

REFLECTION

One thing I carried for years after my financial demise was guilt. I had let down my friends, my family and myself. Guilt robs us of our self-esteem, confidence, energy — everything we need if we are to get back on the bike and ride again.

It had been around six months; I'd begun to find my feet working on commission. I visited a small company that sold mirrors. It had been started by one man on a market stall and was now run by his sons, who sold their wares all over the UK.

The atmosphere in their office was really relaxed. I guess the fact that I was still carrying the guilt of my demise was pretty obvious. Then, one of the brothers gave me a priceless piece of wisdom.

He said, 'You've told us that you dealt with most of your suppliers for many years, and it strikes me that they did pretty well out of you until recently. If you were to offer me a chance to sell you £5,000 worth of mirrors every month for the next five years, and I was going to earn £2,000 every time, but you warned me that after five years you would go bust, owing me £10,000, would I take the deal? You bet I would. It would have cost me £10,000 to earn £120,000. That's good business in anyone's book'.

His words were the kick in the backside I needed. Chances are he has forgotten them, but I haven't, and never will.

CONCLUSION
My Most Important Meeting

I was on my way to Glasgow but had to call in to see a potentially huge client in Liverpool on the way. I had to park my car on a side street some distance away. Getting out, I noticed a girl sitting in a doorway on the ther side of the street. As I walked to the parking pay-point, she asked me if I had any spare change.

'No, sorry', I replied. But having paid my parking fee, I was left with just a small amount of change. I crossed the road to give it to her. I am always reminded of Mother Teresa's words in these situations where she challenged us to help someone feel they are not alone. As I gave her the money, I bent down to speak with her.

'Why are you here?' I asked. 'You're not going to get much money. This street is really quiet. Wouldn't you be better off in a busy street?'

'I'm ashamed', she said. 'I don't want people to know I've come to this'.

She told me that she was trying to get the money together to buy some clean underwear. As she spoke, a single tear flowed down her cheek; that tear moved me deeply. She wasn't begging because it was easy money; she had nowhere to go and no one to turn to.

As I lay in my hotel room that night, pondering the important meetings I'd had that day, it suddenly hit me that they mattered not a jot. The most important one by far was that one in a doorway. It changed my life. No one should have to face what that girl faced. All it would take would be for people to care a little more for people like her not to be alone — to be warm and know that someone is there for them.

The moral of the story? For all of us who seek to do well, just remember that money is just *do-good tokens*. If we all saw it as that, the world would be a better, kinder place.

Her name was Nicola. I hope you are warm and safe and happy, Nicola. I should have done more. We all should.

AEROPLANES AND POTATOES

In my time, I've made a lot of money, and I've lost a lot of money. I've had flash cars, even aeroplanes, but I also know what it's like to be on the floor. Not so long ago, I hit financial rock bottom. I had to choose between putting petrol in my car or paying child maintenance due to my ex. It wasn't much of a choice, so on a very hot September day, I cycled 30 miles on my old bike that had no brakes and was stuck in one gear.

On the way home, with just pennies in my pocket, I stopped to pick up a potato that had fallen from a farm tractor. As I picked it up, I was glad I was in a country lane, and there was no one to see me. I was ashamed. But at least now I had something for dinner.

Let me ask you a question. When we look back, what were the times when we learned the most? Were they the good times when everything was going our way? Or were they the times when we were having a tough time? I believe that success is a great teacher, but failure is a better one. That potato taught me more than any aeroplane adventure ever could. It taught me humility and showed me that I'd been persuing the wrong dreams all along. It made me realise that it's the rocks in the road that make the journey worthwhile. When I look back at those rocks, what do you think I see?

Stepping stones.

Most of us have goals. Nothing wrong with that; they're useful tools to help us achieve what we want. But what happens when those goals seem to elude us no matter how hard we strive? When that happens, those goals that are meant to help us are whispering to us day after day, 'You're failing, you're failing'.

So how do we avoid it? Sometimes we can't.

What about if we cheat? Move the goalposts? Change the tape measure?

Every business, whether its owners know it or not, has a balance sheet. Can anyone give me a half a dozen words on what a balance sheet actually is? How about...a picture in time of what a business holds as assets as opposed to what it owes?

Balance sheets are always expressed in terms of money. Pounds . . . dollars . . . euros. But what if we could change that pound sign or dollar or euro sign for something else?

Ask yourself this: Why did you get into business in the first place? To be rich? To be free? There are countless reasons on the surface as to why anyone goes into business, but if we keep asking *why*, eventually we get down to one word — happiness.

For almost four decades, I was constantly chasing the dollar. Nothing else mattered. I had to lose not one, not two or even three, but FOUR fortunes before I realised just how wrong I was. Why not cut out the middleman and go straight to happy? Don't pass 'go', don't collect £200, just go straight to happiness. Happiness is a decision!

Instead of concentrating on your financial balance sheet, draw up a happiness balance sheet, not just for your business but for yourself. Help your family to create their own. Do the same for your staff. If you can deliver happiness, you will find your own.

Ladies and gentlemen, since I finally learned my lesson, I've been called 'the Man of Joy' I went to hell and back to get that title, but you don't have to.

If the rocks in my road can help you find your way past yours, turn them into stepping stones. All you have to do is reach out.

AFTERWORD

There are countless others who are in their own Lonely Seat, some ready to put an arm around someone else, others desperate to receive one. No one can teach us what it is like in the boss's chair, and only those who have sat in it can understand.

What lesson do I draw from everything I have been through? The key to happiness does not lie in money and trinkets. It lies in the hand we give to others and in the contribution we make. **Be audacious, be brave; whatever you do, never sacrifice your integrity, but most of all . . . be kind.**

THE END. OR IS IT?

What did I learn from my rollercoaster journey? What would have been different if I had known then what I know now?

There were quite a few things that I got right, but in honesty, that was probably more by luck than judgement. I probably got just as many things wrong! I'd like to think that if I had my time again, I'd keep the good traits and lose the bad ones, but that's easier said than done. We cling onto them so tightly that the only way we can let go is to have them surgically removed. Even if we realise at the time (and it's by no means certain that we will) that they are not serving us, we will refuse to let go. Who's to say that I wouldn't repeat my old behavioural patterns when put back into the same circumstances? There are solutions to that dilemma. Now I am aware of the danger, I can guard against it by making sure that I have people around me who will call me out on such behaviour. Non-sycophantic people who don't need my money or favour, who love me enough to tell me the truth. History is filled with well-known entertainers who died before their time because no one close to them loved them enough to tell them they were being a jerk!

All of that said, I will finish off by listing what I got right and what I got wrong. I'll leave it to you to decide if you think, given what you have read in this book, that I am being honest with myself. But most important of all, when you look at my list of good traits that helped me grow more than one successful business and bad traits that led to their demise, ask yourself how many apply to you.

GOOD TRAITS

These are the seven pillars upon which everything I have ever succeeded in are based.

Audaciousness
Daring to be different. For me, following the crowd meant to be only average, at best.

Bravery
Always prepared to experiment and take the consequences for a bad decision.

Honesty

Not just in the broadest sense but also in terms of self-honesty, acknowledging my mistakes and always accepting responsibility for my actions or lack of them.

Imagination

Einstein said that everything we see was once imagined. Imagination is the key to everything. It breeds creativity and faith that something will work out. Imagination breeds confidence and allows us to see things from previously unconsidered perspectives.

Determination

You have not lost until you give in. No one, but NO ONE, ever got anywhere by giving up.

Empathy

The ability to understand how the other person is feeling and why they are feeling that way . . . an unrivalled selling and management tool.

Integrity

Integrity is what we do when we think no one is looking. It is arguably the attribute I hold most precious. It underpins everything I ever do. Sometimes its light has faded, but anything carved in the stone of integrity will last far beyond the years of humankind.

Now for the bad traits: the four wrecking balls that more than once led to my demise.

BAD TRAITS

Blind empathy

Yes, I know I have listed it in my good traits, but empathy is a double-edged sword. If we over-empathise, then we put the needs of others ahead of our own. If we do that too often, then our ability to provide for those who look to us for their wellbeing or livelihood can be seriously impaired.

Picture this . . . you are on a world cruise with your family. The ship has struck rocks and sunk. You are bobbing up and down in the water with your family. An empty life raft floats past. Whom should you put into the life raft first? Most people instinctively answer 'my children', but how can you do that from your position in the water? When you try to push them up, you will simply go down instead. Far better to get yourself into the raft; then you will be in a position of strength to help the others.

Misplaced trust

I am a trusting soul and always like to give someone the benefit of the doubt, but there was always one notable exception. I was never good at delegating, and delegation is based upon trust. Trust that the other person will carry out a particular task properly and efficiently.

I always considered myself to be the best at everything in my companies. Chances are I wasn't, but even if it were true, I never learned the lesson that so long as someone did the job adequately albeit more slowly, then I would have been free to make better use of my time elsewhere. To coin a phrase, I would've been working *on* the business instead of *in* the business.

Wanting to be liked

This I placed above anything else I did. Instead of calling out bad behaviour, I let it go. I accepted poor work ethics because I wanted to be liked. I let others take advantage of me because I wanted to be liked.

But here's the thing: in chasing this holy grail of *wanting to be liked*, I put my whole business at risk. Through not firing people who did not perform *because I wanted to be liked.* Through not insisting on people giving a fair day's work and trying to make up for this lack by working overnight myself to make up for the lack of production *because I wanted to be liked*, I drove the company into the ground. Everyone lost their job.

My actions in wanting to be liked achieved the very opposite of what I intended.

Seeing money as the be-all and end-all

I had to lose four fortunes before I learned that my happiness didn't lie at the end of a financial rainbow. The more I had, the more I wanted. I didn't want money for the good I could do with it, I didn't even want it for the trappings it could bring; I just wanted money for its own sake. Scrooge or what?

Finally, I've just noticed in the last paragraph that I wrote I didn't even want money for the trappings it could bring. And that is the very essence of what money can become . . . like an addiction, it sneaks up on us, and before we know it, we are trapped in its clutches. Nothing matters other than the next fix! We are surrounded by trappings that have become a cage. The bars of our cage keep us trapped inside but just as importantly prevent others from getting close to us for our fear that they may want to take our precious money.

I make no apology for repeating myself, because this is important. Do not bother passing go. Do not bother passing go to collect yet another $200. Just go direct to happy. Never rely on that middleman called money. He should always be your servant, not your master.

A Final Thought

It's not the situation
You find that you are in,
It's the thoughts you have about it
That have you in a spin.

Take a moment, step aside
Accept what's gone is gone,
Spot your thoughts then change them
Is the way that you move on.

Take time to stop, to change your view
When something turns out wrong.
Could it be the kick in the rear
You needed all along?

From now on, stop playing the victim
It's a role that serves you badly.
See beyond the door of gloom
The world will treat you gladly.

It happened for a reason,
Whatever it may be.
Take it, grasp it, turn it, squeeze it,
You'll be amazed at what you see.

ABOUT THE AUTHOR

Described as a serial entrepreneur, Keith set up his first enterprise whilst still at school. By his late twenties, he'd established a successful business, growing exponentially against a tide of recession. Other businesses followed with varying degrees of success (and failure). He maintains that all of them brought lessons, some learned at the time, others only after years of hindsight. Nowadays, as the CEO of a successful consulting company, Keith has enthusiasm for business, and indeed life, that is undiminished.

As well as an entrepreneur and writer, Keith is an accomplished musician and the chairman of a local football club. He gives his time to his old school to show the youngsters (as he puts it) . . . 'If an idiot like me can do it, so can you'. He has two sons and lives with his incredibly tolerant wife in Shropshire.

Printed in Great Britain
by Amazon